Bible Verses For Born-Again Believers

The Bible Study Series, Volume 1

Justin Horn

Published by Justin Horn, 2024.

BIBLE VERSES FOR BORN-AGAIN BELIEVERS

First edition. May 5, 2024.

ISBN: 979-8224125784

Written by Justin Horn.

Table of Contents

Introduction

THE BIBLE, SUCH AN amazing collection of books. Among it's pages can be found the most precious and profound truths in all the world. Throughout the ages, it's contents has guided many a soul to the path of everlasting life. There are so many interesting things about scripture, it's not just a book of rules to live by; although it is a great moral compass. The bible also contains the true history of our origins, the events of the past, it records the miraculous dealings of God and man, there are also many fulfilled prophecies as well as prophecies yet to come. It answers some of Life's most important questions; such as where do we come from, how did all of earth's languages arise, what is my purpose, and do I have value?

I don't know about you but I like making lists, especially when it comes to bible topics. Sure I like reading the bible regularly, but there's something about searching out and comparing the verses from different books of the bible on various topics that gets me excited. It's one of the quickest way new converts can learn bible doctrine and answer important religious questions. Some things in the bible are very consistent throughout all the books, such as moral issues; such as thou shalt not steal. Other things have changed over time such as the dietary laws, the prohibition on wearing mixed fabric, and the animal sacrificial system. The bible has and will always be a fountain of invaluable knowledge.

Sometimes you can't get the full counsel of God by reading just one book of the bible. The book Ruth for example doesn't mention the name of God in any of it's chapters. Another example is Philemon, although it's a valuable book of scripture, it doesn't describe what happens in the afterlife. False doctrine can arise when you believe one part of scripture but not the other parts of scripture. For instance the heresy of soul sleep may arise if one reads Ecclesiastes without taking into account what Jesus says about hell in the gospels. Thus we must take into account other portions of scripture when trying to understand difficult or confusing passages, as well as the context. Also remember that we need the Holy Spirit in order to understand spiritual truths (1 Cor 2:13-14). The following are two examples of comparing scriptures and/or topical study.

1Co 2:13 Which things also we speak, not in the words which man's wisdom teacheth, but which the Holy Ghost teacheth; comparing spiritual things with spiritual.

Luk 24:27 And beginning at Moses and all the prophets, he expounded unto them in all the scriptures the things concerning himself.

In this book will discuss Christian Theology, virtues mentioned in the scriptures, the fruits of the Spirit, and many more benevolent topics.

I sincerely hope you enjoy reading Vol. 1 of Bible Verses for Born-Again Christians.

Chapter 1: Theology

40+ Names/Titles of God

This one is pretty self explanatory. While some of God's names/titles are descriptions of his attributes (i.e. love, jealous, I AM, Strength of Israel), others are descriptions of his position, such as King of kings, Lords of lords, and Creator. Still other names/titles reference what he does (Counselor, Shepherd).

I would advise the reader to be careful how you handle God's name. The third commandment is "Thou shalt not take the name of the LORD thy God in vain...". OMG is a common saying in America today and most people don't even realize what they are doing when they say it. This is called blasphemy and it was punished by death in the Old Testament; so please reverence the holy names of the Father, The Son, and the Holy Spirit. Also note that it is by it the name of Jesus that people are saved and demons flee. Also I may add another possible way of taking the Lord's name in vain is to say I'm a Christian, but to continue to live in unrepentant sin.

Have you ever looked into the Hebrew language of God's names. There's Jehovah-Rapha (the God who heals), and Jehovah-Jirah (the Lord will provide), Elohim (God the Creator), El Sali (the Lord is my strength), as well as El Shaddai (the All-sufficient One, the Almighty). This is but a tiny sample of Hebrew names of the Lord.

Fun Fact: Every time you breath, you are in effect saying God's name: Inhale (YH) and Exhale (WH).

This is just a partial list, so if you so desire, it should not be too difficult to acquire a more complete list. May I recommend John Paul Jackson's CD " I AM: 365 Names of God".

Gen 1:1 In the beginning **God** created the heaven and the earth.

Exo 3:14 And God said unto Moses, **I AM THAT I AM**: and he said, Thus shalt thou say unto the children of Israel, I AM hath sent me unto you.

Exo 6:3 And I appeared unto Abraham, unto Isaac, and unto Jacob, by *the name of* God Almighty, but by my name **JEHOVAH** was I not known to them.

Exo 34:14 For thou shalt worship no other god: for the LORD, whose name *is* **Jealous**, *is* a jealous God:

1Sa 15:29 And also the **Strength of Israel** will not lie nor repent: for he *is* not a man, that he should repent.

Psa 68:4 Sing unto God, sing praises to his name: extol him that rideth upon the heavens by his name **JAH**, and rejoice before him.

Ecc 12:1 Remember now thy **Creator** in the days of thy youth, while the evil days come not, nor the years draw nigh, when thou shalt say, I have no pleasure in them;

Isa 7:14 Therefore the Lord himself shall give you a sign; Behold, a virgin shall conceive, and bear a son, and shall call his name **Immanuel**.

Isa 9:6 For unto us a child is born, unto us a son is given: and the government shall be upon his shoulder: and his name shall be called **Wonderful, Counsellor, The mighty God, The everlasting Father, The Prince of Peace**.

Dan 7:13 I saw in the night visions, and, behold, *one* like the **Son of man** came with the clouds of heaven, and came to the **Ancient of days**, and they brought him near before him.

Hos 2:16 And it shall be at that day, saith the LORD, *that* thou shalt call me **Ishi**; and shalt call me no more Baali.

Zec 6:12 And speak unto him, saying, Thus speaketh the LORD of hosts, saying, Behold the man whose name *is* **The BRANCH**; and he shall grow up out of his place, and he shall build the temple of the LORD:

Mal 4:2 But unto you that fear my name shall the **Sun of righteousness** arise with healing in his wings; and ye shall go forth, and grow up as calves of the stall.

Mat 1:21 And she shall bring forth a son, and thou shalt call his name **JESUS**: for he shall save his people from their sins.

Mar 14:61 But he held his peace, and answered nothing. Again the high priest asked him, and said unto him, Art thou **the Christ**, the **Son of the Blessed**?

Luk 5:34 And he said unto them, Can ye make the children of the bridechamber fast, while the **bridegroom** is with them?

Jon 1:9 And he said unto them, I *am* an Hebrew; and I fear **the LORD**, the God of heaven, which hath made the sea and the dry *land*.

Joh 1:1 In the beginning was **the Word**, and the Word was with God, and the Word was God.

Joh 6:35 And Jesus said unto them, I am the **bread of life**: he that cometh to me shall never hunger; and he that believeth on me shall never thirst.

Joh 10:9 I am **the door**: by me if any man enter in, he shall be saved, and shall go in and out, and find pasture.

Joh 14:6 Jesus saith unto him, I am **the way, the truth, and the life**: no man cometh unto the Father, but by me.

Eph 1:6 To the praise of the glory of his grace, wherein he hath made us accepted in **the beloved**.

1Pe 2:25 For ye were as sheep going astray; but are now returned unto the **Shepherd and Bishop** of your souls.

1Jn 5:7 For there are three that bear record in heaven, **the Father, the Word, and the Holy Ghost**: and these three are one.

Rev 1:8 I am **Alpha and Omega**, the beginning and the ending, saith the Lord, which is, and which was, and which is to come, **the Almighty**.

Rev 3:14 And unto the angel of the church of the Laodiceans write; These things saith **the Amen**, the faithful and true witness, the beginning of the creation of God;

Rev 19:16 And he hath on *his* vesture and on his thigh a name written, **KING OF KINGS, AND LORD OF LORDS**.

Rev 22:16 I Jesus have sent mine angel to testify unto you these things in the churches. I am **the root and the offspring of David,** *and* **the bright and morning star.**

Attributes of God

GOD'S ATTRIBUTES IS such an important study, for Christians ought to know who the true God is; as it is written, "...they that worship him must worship *him* in spirit and in truth." (John 4:24). Some of God's attributes stem from his character, while other's on this list are from his Qualities.

So why is it important to know God's attributes? Well for one we are supposed to be followers of Jesus (God), therefore we should want to know his attributes in order to mimic him. Also It's important to know the Lord's attributes (love, merciful, Just, holy, etc) because it helps ones prayer life. Now what do I mean by that? For me at least, I like to recite some of God's attributes when I pray; it reminds me of who God is.

In the following section I'm going to list twelve attributes of God. Please note that this is not a complete list (by all means check out other sources for a more in depth study); this study is just to whet the appetite so to speak and get a basic understanding of the Lord Jesus.

1. Eternal: Without beginning or end

Psa 90:2 Before the mountains were brought forth, or ever thou hadst formed the earth and the world, even from everlasting to everlasting, thou *art* God.

2. Unchanging

Mal 3:6 For I *am* the LORD, I change not; therefore ye sons of Jacob are not consumed.

3. Omniscient: All-Knowing

Isa_46:10 Declaring the end from the beginning, and from ancient times *the things* that are not *yet* done, saying, My counsel shall stand, and I will do all my pleasure:

Joh_21:17 He saith unto him the third time, Simon, *son* of Jonas, lovest thou me? Peter was grieved because he said unto him the third time, Lovest thou me? And he said unto him, Lord, thou knowest all things; thou knowest that I love thee. Jesus saith unto him, Feed my sheep.

4. Omnipotent: All-Powerful

Col 1:16 For by him were all things created, that are in heaven, and that are in earth, visible and invisible, whether *they be* thrones, or dominions, or principalities, or powers: all things were created by him, and for him:

Col 1:17 And he is before all things, and by him all things consist.

Rev_19:6 And I heard as it were the voice of a great multitude, and as the voice of many waters, and as the voice of mighty thunderings, saying, Alleluia: for the Lord God omnipotent reigneth.

5. Omnipresent: Everywhere

Psa 139:8 If I ascend up into heaven, thou *art* there: if I make my bed in hell, behold, thou *art there*.

Jer 23:24 Can any hide himself in secret places that I shall not see him? saith the LORD. Do not I fill heaven and earth? saith the LORD.

6. Sinless (Righteous): Free from Wickedness and Sin

Deu 32:4 *He is* the Rock, his work *is* perfect: for all his ways *are* judgment: a God of truth and without iniquity, just and right *is* he.

1Jn 3:5 And ye know that he was manifested to take away our sins; and in him is no sin.

7. Loving

Joh 15:13 Greater love hath no man than this, that a man lay down his life for his friends.

1Jn 4:8 He that loveth not knoweth not God; for God is love.

8. Long suffering: Patient, slow to anger

Joe 2:13 And rend your heart, and not your garments, and turn unto the LORD your God: for he *is* gracious and merciful, slow to anger, and of great kindness, and repenteth him of the evil.

2Pe 3:9 The Lord is not slack concerning his promise, as some men count slackness; but is longsuffering to us-ward, not willing that any should perish, but that all should come to repentance.

9.Merciful

Psa 103:8 The LORD *is* merciful and gracious, slow to anger, and plenteous in mercy.

Psa 136:2 O give thanks unto the God of gods: for his mercy *endureth* for ever.

10.Holy

Rev 4:8 And the four beasts had each of them six wings about *him;* and *they were* full of eyes within: and they rest not day and night, saying, Holy, holy, holy, Lord God Almighty, which was, and is, and is to come.

11. Just

Neh 9:33 Howbeit thou *art* just in all that is brought upon us; for thou hast done right, but we have done wickedly:

12. True

Joh 14:6 Jesus saith unto him, I am the way, the truth, and the life: no man cometh unto the Father, but by me.

2Co 1:18 But *as* God *is* true, our word toward you was not yea and nay.

30+ Reasons I believe Jesus is Divine

ONE OF THE MOST IMPORTANT doctrines of the Christian faith is the teaching that Jesus is God. While other religions teach that Jesus was a prophet (as in Islam) or good moral teacher (as in Atheism); Christianity, however holds that he was much more than a mere man. Some religions such as in Jehovah's witness or 7th day Adventists claim Jesus is Micheal the archangel (although perhaps not all adherents of said religions), while others although admitting Christ' divinity, will also say they can attain godhood or that all creation is god (Mormonism/Hinduism). Only one claim can be true. Which one is it? Read the bible and find out for yourself.

Jesus' divinity is also one of the easiest doctrines to prove, basically because there are so many verses that imply his Godhood. How about I go ahead and rattle off some; he forgives sin, his names (Emmanuel, the Mighty God, everlasting Father, the resurrection and the life, I AM, etc), his countless miracles, Thomas called his God, God called him God (Heb 1:8), Jesus thought it not robbery to be equal with God, nothing was made without him, knows all things, and he accepted worshiped, just to name a small sample.

Answering some objections

As stated earlier there are some groups of people who outright reject Jesus' divinity; they make some pretty ridiculous arguments. I will go ahead and take a moment or two to address four of the most common arguments/scriptures.

1. Nowhere in the bible is Jesus called "God the Son".

While this is true *gasp*, it is also very unreasonable to cling to a belief just because God chose not to put that exact phrase in the bible. We see that Jesus is called capital G God in multiple places of scripture (Isaiah 9, John 1, and 20, Hebrews 1). And pretty much every Christian, (well at least most) knows Jesus as the Son. This is an argument from silence, and as such is not the most impressive way to convince someone of something.

2. A very popular argument (common among Muslim adherents), is the statement "Where in the bible does Jesus say "I am God, worship me"?

Well, we already deducted that the bible calls Jesus God four times at least, plus we also see multiple instances in scripture of Jesus being worshiped, the bible does not say that Jesus rebuked those that worshiped him therefore he accepted worship. Plus in John 8:58 Jesus claims to be the I AM.

3. John 14:28

In this passage Jesus says the Father is greater than himself. Does this therefore mean Jesus isn't God? No, what some people choose to forget or simply don't understand is that Jesus has two natures. A divine nature and a human nature. Only in respect to Jesus *Human Nature* was the Father greater.

4. John 20:17

Just because Jesus refers to the Father as God it doesn't mean that Jesus isn't God, why is that? Just read Hebrews 1:8, it is here that it's either the Father or the Spirit that is calling the Son (Jesus) God. But this does not cancel out their divinity just by calling Jesus God.

I cannot stress this enough to my readers, get this doctrine *right!* What we believe about Jesus can most assuredly affect where we end up in the afterlife. If you worship the wrong Jesus, you worship a false god that cannot save. Only the true Jesus as defined by the scripture can save us. Idolaters will not inherit the kingdom (1 Cor 6:9-10).

REASON #1: JESUS IS Omnipotent!

Joh 15:5 I am the vine, ye *are* the branches: He that abideth in me, and I in him, the same bringeth forth much fruit: **for without me ye can do nothing.**

Php 4:13 **I can do all things through Christ which strengtheneth me.**

Rev 1:8 **I am Alpha and Omega**, the **beginning and the ending**, saith the Lord, which is, and which was, and which is to come, **the Almighty.**

Reason #2: Jesus has Omniscience!

Joh 21:17 He saith unto him the third time, Simon, *son* of Jonas, lovest thou me? Peter was grieved because he said unto him the third time, Lovest thou me? And he said unto him, Lord, **thou knowest all things**; thou knowest that I love thee. Jesus saith unto him, Feed my sheep.

Reason #3: Jesus is Omnipresent!

Mat 28:20 Teaching them to observe all things whatsoever I have commanded you: and, lo, I am with you alway, *even* unto the end of the world. Amen. [Jer 23:24]

Rom 8:9 But ye are not in the flesh, but in the Spirit, if so be that the **Spirit of God** dwell in you. Now if any man have not the **Spirit of Christ**, he is none of his.

Heb 13:5 *Let your* conversation *be* without covetousness; *and be* content with such things as ye have: for he hath said, **I will never leave thee, nor forsake thee.**

Reason #4: Jesus forgave sin.

Mar 2:5 When Jesus saw their faith, he said unto the sick of the palsy, Son, **thy sins be forgiven thee.** [Mark 2:7]

Reason #5: Jesus is Unchanging.

Heb 13:8 Jesus Christ the same yesterday, and to day, and for ever.

Reason #6: Jesus blood is God's blood.

Act 20:28 Take heed therefore unto yourselves, and to all the flock, over the which the Holy Ghost hath made you overseers, to feed the church of **God, which he hath purchased with his own blood.**

Reason #7: Jesus/God is Judge.

Joh 5:22 For the Father judgeth no man, but hath committed all judgment unto the Son:

Psa 50:6 And the heavens shall declare his righteousness: for **God** *is* **judge himself**. Selah.

Reason #8: The lamb.

Gen 22:8 And Abraham said, My son, **God will provide himself a lamb** for a burnt offering: so they went both of them together. See John 1:29

Reason #9: Called God (virtually every instance of capital G-God in the bible refers to the true God).

Isa 9:6 For unto us **a child is born**, unto us a son is given: and the government shall be upon his shoulder: and his name shall be called Wonderful, Counsellor, **The mighty God, The everlasting Father**, The Prince of Peace.

Joh 1:1 In the beginning was the Word, and the Word was with God, and the **Word was God**.

Joh 1:14 And the Word was made flesh, and dwelt among us, (and we beheld his glory, the glory as of the only begotten of the Father,) full of grace and truth.

Joh 1:17 For the law was given by Moses, *but* grace and truth came by Jesus Christ.

Joh 20:28 And Thomas answered and **said unto him, My Lord and my God**.

1Ti 3:16 And without controversy great is the mystery of godliness: **God was manifest in the flesh,** justified in the Spirit, seen of angels, preached unto the Gentiles, believed on in the world, received up into glory.

Heb 1:8 **But unto the Son** *he saith,* **Thy throne, O God,** *is* **for ever** and ever: a sceptre of righteousness *is* the sceptre of thy kingdom.

Reason #10: He is Eternal.

Mic 5:2 But thou, Bethlehem Ephratah, *though* thou be little among the thousands of Judah, *yet* out of thee shall he come forth unto me *that is* to be ruler in Israel; whose goings forth *have been* from of old, **from everlasting.** ^Psa 90:2^

Reason #11: Jesus declared he was God (I Am).

Joh 8:58 Jesus said unto them, Verily, verily, I say unto you, Before Abraham was, **I am.** ^Exodus 3:14^

Reason #12: Jesus believed he was equal to God.

Php 2:6 Who, being in the form of God, **thought it not robbery to be equal with God:**

Reason #13: All things made by Jesus.

Joh 1:3 **All things were made by him**; and without him was not any thing made that was made.

Eph 3:9 And to make all *men* see what *is* the fellowship of the mystery, which from the beginning of the world hath been hid in **God, who created all things by Jesus Christ:**

Col 1:16 For by him were all things created, that are in heaven, and that are in earth, visible and invisible, whether *they be* thrones, or dominions, or principalities, or powers: **all things were created by him, and for him:**

Col 1:17 **And he is before all things, and by him all things consist.**

Heb 1:2 Hath in these last days spoken unto us by *his* Son, whom he hath appointed heir of all things, **by whom also he made the worlds;**

Heb 3:3 **For this *man* was counted worthy of more glory than Moses, inasmuch as he who hath builded the house hath more honour than the house.**

Heb 3:4 **For every house is builded by some *man;* but he that built all things *is* God.**

Reason #14: Called Emmanuel.

Mat 1:23 Behold, a virgin shall be with child, and shall bring forth a son, and they shall call his name **Emmanuel**, which being interpreted is, God with us.

Reason #15: Called Son of Man.

Dan 7:13 I saw in the night visions, and, behold, *one* like the **Son of man** came with the clouds of heaven, and came to the Ancient of days, and they brought him near before him.

Reason #16: Accepted worship.

Luk 24:52 And they worshipped him, and returned to Jerusalem with great joy: Acts 10:25,Rev 22:8-9

Heb 1:5 **For unto which of the angels said he at any time, Thou art my Son,** this day have I begotten thee? And again, I will be to him a Father, and he shall be to me a Son?

Heb 1:6 And again, when he bringeth in the firstbegotten into the world, he saith, And **let all the angels of God worship him.**

Reason #17: Jesus is Saviour.

Tit 1:4 To Titus, *mine* own son after the common faith: Grace, mercy, *and* peace, from God the Father and the Lord Jesus Christ our Saviour. Titus 1:3

Reason #18: Many miracles.

Joh 7:31 And many of the people believed on him, and said, When Christ cometh, will he do more **miracles** than these which this *man* hath done?

Reason #19: Lawgiver.

Mat 5:33 Again, ye have heard that it hath been said by them of old time, Thou shalt not forswear thyself, but shalt perform unto the Lord thine oaths:

Mat 5:34 **But I say unto you, Swear not at all**; neither by heaven; for it is God's throne:

Reason #20: God doesn't share his glory with another, yet he did with Jesus.

Joh 17:5 And now, O Father, glorify thou me with thine own self **with the glory which I had with thee before the world was.** Isaiah 42:8

Reason #21: The rock.

2Sa 22:32 For who *is* God, save the LORD? and **who *is* a rock, save our God?** 1 Cor 10:4

Reason #22: Numerous Trinity verses throughout scripture.

Reason #23: Knew the thoughts of man.

Mat 9:4 And Jesus **knowing their thoughts** said, Wherefore think ye evil in your hearts? 1 kings 8:39

Reason #24: Jesus is sinless.

Rom 3:23 For all have sinned, and come short of the glory of God; 1john 3:5

2Co 5:21 For he hath made him *to be* sin for us, who knew no sin; that we might be made the righteousness of God in him. 2Ch 19:7

1Jn 3:5 And ye know that he was manifested to take away our sins; and in him is no sin.

Reason #25: Appeared multiple times in the Old Testament (covered later).

Dan 3:25 He answered and said, Lo, I see four men loose, walking in the midst of the fire, and they have no hurt; and the form of the fourth is like the **Son of God.** John 9:35

Reason #26: Called Messiah/Christ.

Joh 4:25 The woman saith unto him, I know that **Messias** cometh, which is called **Christ**: when he is come, he will tell us all things.

Joh 4:26 Jesus saith unto her, **I that speak unto thee am *he*.**

Reason #27: Called Lord.

Mat 25:45 Then shall he answer them, saying, Verily I say unto you, Inasmuch as ye did *it* not to one of the least of these, ye did *it* not to me. Proverbs 19:17

Mat 3:3 For this is he that was spoken of by the prophet Esaias, saying, The voice of one crying in the wilderness, Prepare ye the way of **the Lord**, make his paths straight.

Php 2:11 And *that* every tongue should confess that **Jesus Christ *is* Lord**, to the glory of God the Father.

Reason #28: Jesus is light of the world.

Joh 8:12 Then spake Jesus again unto them, saying, **I am the light of the world**: he that followeth me shall not walk in darkness, but shall have the light of life. 1John 1:5

Reason #29: Image of the Father.

Joh 14:9 Jesus saith unto him, Have I been so long time with you, and yet hast thou not known me, Philip? **he that hath seen me hath seen the Father**; and how sayest thou *then,* Shew us the Father?

Reason #30: More verses that suggest Christ's divinity.

Isa 63:5 And I looked, and *there was* none to help; and I wondered that *there was* none to uphold: therefore **mine own arm brought salvation** unto me; and my fury, it upheld me.

Mar 1:1 The beginning of the gospel of Jesus Christ, the **Son of God**;

Luk 8:39 Return to thine own house, and shew how **great things God hath done unto thee**. And he went his way, and published throughout the whole city how great things **Jesus had done unto him**.

Joh 2:19 Jesus answered and said unto them, Destroy this temple, and in three days I will raise it up.

Joh 10:30 **I and *my* Father are one.** 1 John 5:7

Joh 11:25 Jesus said unto her, **I am the resurrection, and the life**: he that believeth in me, though he were dead, yet shall he live:

Joh 11:26 And whosoever liveth and believeth in me shall never die. Believest thou this?

Act 7:59 And they stoned Stephen, calling upon *God,* and saying, Lord Jesus, receive my spirit. **Gal 1:1** Paul, an apostle, (**not of men, neither by man**, but by Jesus Christ, and God the Father, who raised him from the dead;)

Rev 1:6 And hath made us kings and priests unto God and his Father; to him *be* glory and dominion for ever and ever. Amen.

Rev 19:16 And he hath on *his* vesture and on his thigh a name written, **KING OF KINGS, AND LORD OF LORDS.**

Holy Spirit

WHAT CAN BE SAID ABOUT the Holy Spirit? Well number one, He is God. A member of the trinity, along with the Father and Son. He is referred to in the masculine in John chapters 14 and 16. He is not the teachings of Christian Science as Mary Baker Eddy would say. Nor is he an impersonal force as JW's Teach. Nor is he Sun Myung Moon's Wife as the Unification Church taught. I would be very cautious about joining the aforementioned groups of people, because the blasphemy of the Holy Ghost is one of the two sins that are unforgivable. The other being taking the mark of the beast.

What are some of the roles of the Spirit? Here is a small sample of his roles...

- He comforts

- Gives Spiritual gifts

- Convicts of sin

- He guides into all truth

- He Intercedes for us

How do we know He is a person, well in addition to being identified with male pronouns no less that 7 times in a single verse (John 16:13), he also gives orders and makes judgment in the book of Acts, is said to have a mind and make intercession for us in Romans, has a will in 1 Corinthians, and can be grieved as said in Ephesians.

For ease of Lookup I've separated this topic into four categories.

PROVED PERSON HOOD.

Joh 16:13 Howbeit when he, the Spirit of truth, is come, he will guide you into all truth: for he shall not speak of himself; but whatsoever he shall hear, *that* shall he speak: and he will shew you things to come.

Act 5:3 But Peter said, Ananias, why hath Satan filled thine heart to lie to the Holy Ghost, and to keep back *part* of the price of the land?

Act 5:4 Whiles it remained, was it not thine own? and after it was sold, was it not in thine own power? why hast thou conceived this thing in thine heart? thou hast not lied unto men, but unto God.

Act 5:32 And we are his witnesses of these things; and *so is* also the Holy Ghost, whom God hath given to them that obey him.

Act 13:2 As they ministered to the Lord, and fasted, the Holy Ghost said, Separate me Barnabas and Saul for the work whereunto I have called them.

Act 13:4 So they, being sent forth by the Holy Ghost, departed unto Seleucia; and from thence they sailed to Cyprus.

Act 16:6 Now when they had gone throughout Phrygia and the region of Galatia, and were forbidden of the Holy Ghost to preach the word in Asia,

Act 15:28 For it seemed good to the Holy Ghost, and to us, to lay upon you no greater burden than these necessary things;

Act 20:23 Save that the Holy Ghost witnesseth in every city, saying that bonds and afflictions abide me.

Act 21:11 And when he was come unto us, he took Paul's girdle, and bound his own hands and feet, and said, Thus saith the Holy Ghost, So shall the Jews at Jerusalem bind the man that owneth this girdle, and shall deliver *him* into the hands of the Gentiles.

Act 28:25 And when they agreed not among themselves, they departed, after that Paul had spoken one word, Well spake the Holy Ghost by Esaias the prophet unto our fathers,

Rom 8:26 Likewise the Spirit also helpeth our infirmities: for we know not what we should pray for as we ought: but the Spirit itself maketh intercession for us with groanings which cannot be uttered.

Rom 8:27 And he that searcheth the hearts knoweth what *is* the mind of the Spirit, because he maketh intercession for the saints according to *the will of God.*

1Co 2:11 For what man knoweth the things of a man, save the spirit of man which is in him? even so the things of God knoweth no man, but the Spirit of God.

1Co 12:11 But all these worketh that one and the selfsame Spirit, dividing to every man severally as he will.

Eph 4:30 And grieve not the holy Spirit of God, whereby ye are sealed unto the day of redemption.

Heb 3:7 Wherefore (as the Holy Ghost saith, To day if ye will hear his voice,

Heb 10:15 *Whereof* the Holy Ghost also is a witness to us: for after that he had said before,

Rev 3:22 He that hath an ear, let him hear what the Spirit saith unto the churches.

ROLES AND FUNCTIONS.

Exo 31:3 And I have filled him with the spirit of God, in wisdom, and in understanding, and in knowledge, and in all manner of workmanship,

1Sa 19:23 And he went thither to Naioth in Ramah: and the Spirit of God was upon him also, and he went on, and prophesied, until he came to Naioth in Ramah.

Job 33:4 The Spirit of God hath made me, and the breath of the Almighty hath given me life.

Eze 11:24 Afterwards the spirit took me up, and brought me in a vision by the Spirit of God into Chaldea, to them of the captivity. So the vision that I had seen went up from me.

Mat 1:18 Now the birth of Jesus Christ was on this wise: When as his mother Mary was espoused to Joseph, before they came together, she was found with child of the Holy Ghost.

Mat 12:28 But if I cast out devils by the Spirit of God, then the kingdom of God is come unto you.

Mar 13:11 But when they shall lead *you,* and deliver you up, take no thought beforehand what ye shall speak, neither do ye premeditate: but whatsoever shall be given you in that hour, that speak ye: for it is not ye that speak, but the Holy Ghost.

Luk 4:1 And Jesus being full of the Holy Ghost returned from Jordan, and was led by the Spirit into the wilderness,

Joh 14:26 But the Comforter, *which is* the Holy Ghost, whom the Father will send in my name, he shall teach you all things, and bring all things to your remembrance, whatsoever I have said unto you.

Act 1:2 Until the day in which he was taken up, after that he through the Holy Ghost had given commandments unto the apostles whom he had chosen:

Act 1:8 But ye shall receive power, after that the Holy Ghost is come upon you: and ye shall be witnesses unto me both in Jerusalem, and in all Judaea, and in Samaria, and unto the uttermost part of the earth.

Act 2:4 And they were all filled with the Holy Ghost, and began to speak with other tongues, as the Spirit gave them utterance.

Act 19:6 And when Paul had laid *his* hands upon them, the Holy Ghost came on them; and they spake with tongues, and prophesied.

Rom 5:5 And hope maketh not ashamed; because the love of God is shed abroad in our hearts by the Holy Ghost which is given unto us.

Rom 8:14 For as many as are led by the Spirit of God, they are the sons of God.

Rom 14:17 For the kingdom of God is not meat and drink; but righteousness, and peace, and joy in the Holy Ghost.

Rom 15:13 Now the God of hope fill you with all joy and peace in believing, that ye may abound in hope, through the power of the Holy Ghost.

Rom 15:19 Through mighty signs and wonders, by the power of the Spirit of God; so that from Jerusalem, and round about unto Illyricum, I have fully preached the gospel of Christ.

1Co 2:13 Which things also we speak, not in the words which man's wisdom teacheth, but which the Holy Ghost teacheth; comparing spiritual things with spiritual.

1Co 2:14 But the natural man receiveth not the things of the Spirit of God: for they are foolishness unto him: neither can he know *them,* because they are spiritually discerned.

Gal 5:18 But if ye be led of the Spirit, ye are not under the law.

Eph 1:13 In whom ye also *trusted,* after that ye heard the word of truth, the gospel of your salvation: in whom also after that ye believed, ye were sealed with that holy Spirit of promise,

1Th 1:5 For our gospel came not unto you in word only, but also in power, and in the Holy Ghost, and in much assurance; as ye know what manner of men we were among you for your sake.

1Th 1:6 And ye became followers of us, and of the Lord, having received the word in much affliction, with joy of the Holy Ghost:

Heb 2:4 God also bearing *them* witness, both with signs and wonders, and with divers miracles, and gifts of the Holy Ghost, according to his own will?

2Pe 1:21 For the prophecy came not in old time by the will of man: but holy men of God spake *as they were* moved by the Holy Ghost.

Jud 1:20 But ye, beloved, building up yourselves on your most holy faith, praying in the Holy Ghost,

TRINITY VERSES.

Mar 12:36 For David himself said by the Holy Ghost, The LORD said to my Lord, Sit thou on my right hand, till I make thine enemies thy footstool.

Luk 3:22 And the Holy Ghost descended in a bodily shape like a dove upon him, and a voice came from heaven, which said, Thou art my beloved Son; in thee I am well pleased.

Luk 12:12 For the Holy Ghost shall teach you in the same hour what ye ought to say.

Rom 15:16 That I should be the minister of Jesus Christ to the Gentiles, ministering the gospel of God, that the offering up of the Gentiles might be acceptable, being sanctified by the Holy Ghost.

MISC.

Gen 1:2 And the earth was without form, and void; and darkness *was* upon the face of the deep. And the Spirit of God moved upon the face of the waters.

Gen 41:38 And Pharaoh said unto his servants, Can we find *such a one* as this *is,* a man in whom the Spirit of God *is?*

Num 24:2 And Balaam lifted up his eyes, and he saw Israel abiding *in his tents* according to their tribes; and the spirit of God came upon him.

Job 27:3 All the while my breath *is* in me, and the spirit of God *is* in my nostrils;

Psa 51:11 Cast me not away from thy presence; and take not thy holy spirit from me.

Isa 63:10 But they rebelled, and vexed his holy Spirit: therefore he was turned to be their enemy, *and* he fought against them.

Mat 3:11 I indeed baptize you with water unto repentance: but he that cometh after me is mightier than I, whose shoes I am not worthy to bear: he shall baptize you with the Holy Ghost, and *with* fire:

Mat 12:32 And whosoever speaketh a word against the Son of man, it shall be forgiven him: but whosoever speaketh against the Holy Ghost, it shall not be forgiven him, neither in this world, neither in the *world* to come.

Mar 3:29 But he that shall blaspheme against the Holy Ghost hath never forgiveness, but is in danger of eternal damnation:

Luk 1:15 For he shall be great in the sight of the Lord, and shall drink neither wine nor strong drink; and he shall be filled with the Holy Ghost, even from his mother's womb.

Luk 1:41 And it came to pass, that, when Elisabeth heard the salutation of Mary, the babe leaped in her womb; and Elisabeth was filled with the Holy Ghost:

Luk 11:13 If ye then, being evil, know how to give good gifts unto your children: how much more shall *your* heavenly Father give the Holy Spirit to them that ask him?

Luk 12:10 And whosoever shall speak a word against the Son of man, it shall be forgiven him: but unto him that blasphemeth against the Holy Ghost it shall not be forgiven.

Joh 7:39 (But this spake he of the Spirit, which they that believe on him should receive: for the Holy Ghost was not yet *given;* because that Jesus was not yet glorified.)

Joh 20:22 And when he had said this, he breathed on *them,* and saith unto them, Receive ye the Holy Ghost:

Act 1:5 For John truly baptized with water; but ye shall be baptized with the Holy Ghost not many days hence.

Act 2:38 Then Peter said unto them, Repent, and be baptized every one of you in the name of Jesus Christ for the remission of sins, and ye shall receive the gift of the Holy Ghost.

Act 4:31 And when they had prayed, the place was shaken where they were assembled together; and they were all filled with the Holy Ghost, and they spake the word of God with boldness.

Act 6:3 Wherefore, brethren, look ye out among you seven men of honest report, full of the Holy Ghost and wisdom, whom we may appoint over this business.

Act 7:51 Ye stiffnecked and uncircumcised in heart and ears, ye do always resist the Holy Ghost: as your fathers *did,* so *do* ye.

Act 8:15 Who, when they were come down, prayed for them, that they might receive the Holy Ghost:

Act 8:17 Then laid they *their* hands on them, and they received the Holy Ghost.

Act 9:17 And Ananias went his way, and entered into the house; and putting his hands on him said, Brother Saul, the Lord, *even* Jesus, that appeared unto thee in the way as thou camest, hath sent me, that thou mightest receive thy sight, and be filled with the Holy Ghost.

Act 10:44 While Peter yet spake these words, the Holy Ghost fell on all them which heard the word.

Act 10:45 And they of the circumcision which believed were astonished, as many as came with Peter, because that on the Gentiles also was poured out the gift of the Holy Ghost.

Act 10:47 Can any man forbid water, that these should not be baptized, which have received the Holy Ghost as well as we?

Act 11:15 And as I began to speak, the Holy Ghost fell on them, as on us at the beginning.

Act 11:16 Then remembered I the word of the Lord, how that he said, John indeed baptized with water; but ye shall be baptized with the Holy Ghost.

Act 13:52 And the disciples were filled with joy, and with the Holy Ghost.

1Co 3:16 Know ye not that ye are the temple of God, and *that* the Spirit of God dwelleth in you?

1Co 6:19 What? know ye not that your body is the temple of the Holy Ghost *which is* in you, which ye have of God, and ye are not your own?

1Co 7:40 But she is happier if she so abide, after my judgment: and I think also that I have the Spirit of God.

1Co 12:3 Wherefore I give you to understand, that no man speaking by the Spirit of God calleth Jesus accursed: and *that* no man can say that Jesus is the Lord, but by the Holy Ghost.

2Co 6:6 By pureness, by knowledge, by longsuffering, by kindness, by the Holy Ghost, by love unfeigned,

1Th 4:8 He therefore that despiseth, despiseth not man, but God, who hath also given unto us his holy Spirit.

Tit 3:5 Not by works of righteousness which we have done, but according to his mercy he saved us, by the washing of regeneration, and renewing of the Holy Ghost;

Heb 9:8 The Holy Ghost this signifying, that the way into the holiest of all was not yet made manifest, while as the first tabernacle was yet standing:

1Jn 4:2 Hereby know ye the Spirit of God: Every spirit that confesseth that Jesus Christ is come in the flesh is of God:

Monotheism

MONOTHEISM IS THE BELIEF that their is only one God. Among the world religions there are three notable ones that teach this doctrine; Judaism, Islam, and Christianity. Although the bible mentions other "gods", they are little g gods (there are only a couple or few exceptions to my knowledge where a capital G is referencing anyone or anything other than the true living God). The bible mentions many false gods, which are not the true God but idols, devils, and men set up as judges. In truth their is only one eternal God who is from everlasting, the one who created the universe and all that in them is.

There are many verses that prove Monotheism true and the list provided may not contain all of said verses, but it should be sufficient to prove the point. Believing in Monotheism alone doesn't save, as it is written "...the devils also believe, and tremble." Only sincerely repenting of your sins and then trusting in Jesus' blood to wash away your sins will save you.

Also consider religions such as Islam and Zoroastrianism, they believe in one God, yet they are still in their sin. Monotheism although an important and necessary doctrine of the christian faith, is insufficient in and of itself to make one a christian.

DEU 4:35 UNTO THEE it was shewed, that thou mightest know that the LORD he *is* God; *there is* none else beside him.

Deu 32:39 See now that I, *even* I, *am* he, and *there is* no god with me: I kill, and I make alive; I wound, and I heal: neither *is there any* that can deliver out of my hand.

1Ch 17:20 O LORD, *there is* none like thee, neither *is there any* God beside thee, according to all that we have heard with our ears.

Neh 9:6 Thou, *even* thou, *art* LORD alone; thou hast made heaven, the heaven of heavens, with all their host, the earth, and all *things* that *are* therein, the seas, and all that *is* therein, and thou preservest them all; and the host of heaven worshippeth thee.

Psa 86:10 For thou *art* great, and doest wondrous things: thou *art* God alone.

Isa 43:10 Ye *are* my witnesses, saith the LORD, and my servant whom I have chosen: that ye may know and believe me, and understand that I *am* he: before me there was no God formed, neither shall there be after me.

Isa 43:11 I, *even* I, *am* the LORD; and beside me *there is* no saviour.

Isa 44:6 Thus saith the LORD the King of Israel, and his redeemer the LORD of hosts; I *am* the first, and I *am* the last; and beside me *there is* no God.

Isa 45:5 I *am* the LORD, and *there is* none else, *there is* no God beside me: I girded thee, though thou hast not known me:

Isa 46:9 Remember the former things of old: for I *am* God, and *there is* none else; *I am* God, and *there is* none like me,

Mar 12:29 And Jesus answered him, The first of all the commandments *is*, Hear, O Israel; The Lord our God is one Lord:

Mar 12:32 And the scribe said unto him, Well, Master, thou hast said the truth: for there is one God; and there is none other but he:

Joh 17:3 And this is life eternal, that they might know thee the only true God, and Jesus Christ, whom thou hast sent.

1Co 8:6 But to us *there is but* one God, the Father, of whom *are* all things, and we in him; and one Lord Jesus Christ, by whom *are* all things, and we by him.

Eph_4:6 One God and Father of all, who *is* above all, and through all, and in you all.

1Ti 2:5 For *there is* one God, and one mediator between God and men, the man Christ Jesus;

Jas 2:19 Thou believest that there is one God; thou doest well: the devils also believe, and tremble.

Trinity

THIS DOCTRINE IS AN *essential* doctrine of the Christian faith, for we must worship the Lord in Spirit and truth. Beware of cults that deny the doctrine of the triune nature of the Godhead. Jehovah's witnesses, Christian Science, as well as some 7th day Adventist deny this precious belief. While it is true the word trinity does not appear in scripture there are many passages that mention the idea of the trinity.

So what is the trinity exactly? The trinity is the teaching the our 1 God is comprised of 3 distinct persons, they are not three gods. When this study is taken together with the study on the deity of Christ as well the study on the Holy Spirit (which reveals his person hood) it provides irrefutable proof of the trinity.

Don't be surprised though if some people don't get it. Although the doctrine of the trinity is easy to explain, it can be hard to comprehend. We must realize that our God is outside of time, space, and matter; and thusly is not restrained from the limits of this universe. If we could comprehend everything about God, would he still be so magnificent? Maybe so, howbeit we may not understand God completely until we get to the other side.

Answering Four Objections to the Trinity

1. The word Trinity isn't in the bible.

The word bible isn't in the bible, does that mean we don't believe the bible? Of coarse not! Guess what is also not in the bible, Omniscient and Omnipresent; does that mean God is not those things? Again of coarse not.

2. Jesus had a beginning (Col 1:15), therefore the trinity is a myth.

Jesus did NOT have a beginning, Micah 5:2 verifies this. If you read down to verse 18 in Colossians (the context) it shows that Jesus was the first begotten from the dead. Ecc 12:7

See also Rev 1:5, 1 Corinthians 15:20.

3. 1 Corinthians 15:28, Jesus submits to the Father, therefore Jesus is not equal to the Father.

By this line of reasoning employees are less valuable than their employers, and wives are inferior to their husbands.

4. 1 Corinthians 11:3 informs us that the head of Christ is God.

This is just like the previous argument. Just because one member of the Godhead submits to the other doesn't mean they are not equal in power, wisdom, ability, etc. In human terms a wife submits to her husband but she is every bit as valuable as he is.

Probably the best place to go in order to defend the precious doctrine of the Trinity is John chapters 14-16. All three persons of the Godhead are mentioned throughout these passages and one would have to do some pretty "impressive" mental gymnastics in order to try and reason out of belief in the trinity there. Why is that? Here are just three examples from these chapters. These are not quotes.

John 14:26- tells us that the Father sends the Comforter in Jesus' name, so is the Father sending himself? The answer is yes (v23) and No.

John 15:26- Again the Comforter is sent by Jesus from the Father and proceeds from the Father.

John 16:13-15- The Spirit doesn't speak of himself but what he hears, and glorifies Jesus. Verse 15 is very interesting here we see that Jesus has all that the Father has and that the Spirit takes from Jesus to shew unto us.

Gen 1:26 And God said, Let us make man in our image, after our likeness: and let them have dominion over the fish of the sea, and over the fowl of the air, and over the cattle, and over all the earth, and over every creeping thing that creepeth upon the earth.

Gen 11:7 Go to, let us go down, and there confound their language, that they may not understand one another's speech.

2Sa 23:2 The Spirit of the LORD spake by me, and his word *was* in my tongue.

2Sa 23:3 The God of Israel said, the Rock of Israel spake to me, He that ruleth over men *must be* just, ruling in the fear of God.

Pro 30:4 Who hath ascended up into heaven, or descended? who hath gathered the wind in his fists? who hath bound the waters in a garment? who hath established all the ends of the earth? what *is* his name, and what *is* his son's name, if thou canst tell?

Isa 48:16 Come ye near unto me, hear ye this; I have not spoken in secret from the beginning; from the time that it was, there *am* I: and now the Lord GOD, and his Spirit, hath sent me.

Zec 3:1 And he shewed me Joshua the high priest standing before the angel of the LORD, and Satan standing at his right hand to resist him.

Zec 3:2 And the LORD said unto Satan, The LORD rebuke thee, O Satan; even the LORD that hath chosen Jerusalem rebuke thee: *is* not this a brand plucked out of the fire?

Mat 3:16 And Jesus, when he was baptized, went up straightway out of the water: and, lo, the heavens were opened unto him, and he saw the Spirit of God descending like a dove, and lighting upon him:

Mat 3:17 And lo a voice from heaven, saying, This is my beloved Son, in whom I am well pleased.

Mat 28:19 Go ye therefore, and teach all nations, baptizing them in the name of the Father, and of the Son, and of the Holy Ghost:

Luk 2:26 And it was revealed unto him by the Holy Ghost, that he should not see death, before he had seen the Lord's Christ.

Joh 14:16 And I will pray the Father, and he shall give you another Comforter, that he may abide with you for ever;

Joh 14:23 Jesus answered and said unto him, If a man love me, he will keep my words: and my Father will love him, and we will come unto him, and make our abode with him.

Act 10:38 How God anointed Jesus of Nazareth with the Holy Ghost and with power: who went about doing good, and healing all that were oppressed of the devil; for God was with him.

Rom 8:9 But ye are not in the flesh, but in the Spirit, if so be that the Spirit of God dwell in you. Now if any man have not the Spirit of Christ, he is none of his.

Rom 15:16 That I should be the minister of Jesus Christ to the Gentiles, ministering the gospel of God, that the offering up of the Gentiles might be acceptable, being sanctified by the Holy Ghost.

2Co 13:14 The grace of the Lord Jesus Christ, and the love of God, and the communion of the Holy Ghost, *be* with you all. Amen.

Gal 4:6 And because ye are sons, God hath sent forth the Spirit of his Son into your hearts, crying, Abba, Father.

Eph 2:18 For through him we both have access by one Spirit unto the Father.

Eph 2:22 In whom ye also are builded together for an habitation of God through the Spirit.

Col 2:2 That their hearts might be comforted, being knit together in love, and unto all riches of the full assurance of understanding, to the acknowledgement of the mystery of God, and of the Father, and of Christ;

Heb 9:14 How much more shall the blood of Christ, who through the eternal Spirit offered himself without spot to God, purge your conscience from dead works to serve the living God?

1Pe 1:2 Elect according to the foreknowledge of God the Father, through sanctification of the Spirit, unto obedience and sprinkling of the blood of Jesus Christ: Grace unto you, and peace, be multiplied.

1Jn 5:7 For there are three that bear record in heaven, the Father, the Word, and the Holy Ghost: and these three are one.

Jud 1:20 But ye, beloved, building up yourselves on your most holy faith, praying in the Holy Ghost,

Jud 1:21 Keep yourselves in the love of God, looking for the mercy of our Lord Jesus Christ unto eternal life.

All three members raised Jesus from the grave.

Rom 6:4 Therefore we are buried with him by baptism into death: that like as Christ was raised up from the dead by the glory of the Father, even so we also should walk in newness of life.

Joh 2:19 Jesus answered and said unto them, Destroy this temple, and in three days I will raise it up.

1Pe 3:18 For Christ also hath once suffered for sins, the just for the unjust, that he might bring us to God, being put to death in the flesh, but quickened by the Spirit:

Christophanies or Possible Ones in OT

WHAT IS A CHRISTOPHANY? A Christophany is the appearance of Jesus in the Old Testament. We see that he is sometimes referred to as the angel of the LORD, as well as other titles. I can see how the title "angel of the Lord" might throw some people off. Some folks may thing wait, ANGEL; I thought Jesus was God. Jesus is God. The word angel can also mean *messenger* among other things.

So who did the angel of the Lord/and/or Lord/and/or captain of the Lord's host appear to in the Old Testament? There was appearances to Abraham, Hagar, and Sarah. Moses and Balaam also encountered an angel of the Lord. When we come to the book of Judges we see that Gideon and Samson's parents have seen an angel of the Lord also. Further on in the bible we find out that King David and Elijah the prophet has seen an angel of the Lord also. Please note that it is not entirely certain that the "angel of the Lord" is in fact pre-incarnate Jesus in the Old Testament. It is just a guess. It's also possible that some of the appearances are Jesus and some are just ordinary angels.

Joshua is the one who encounters the "captain of the LORD'S host", and let's not forget that Jacob wrestled with "a man" which many believe was either God or an angel. Below are some of the possible appearances of Jesus in the Old Testament although there may be more.

---

1. Gen 16:11 And the angel of the LORD said unto her, Behold, thou *art* with child, and shalt bear a son, and shalt call his name Ishmael; because the LORD hath heard thy affliction.

2. Gen 18:1 And the LORD appeared unto him in the plains of Mamre: and he sat in the tent door in the heat of the day;

3. Gen 32:30 And Jacob called the name of the place Peniel: for I have seen God face to face, and my life is preserved.

4. Exo 3:2 And the angel of the LORD appeared unto him in a flame of fire out of the midst of a bush: and he looked, and, behold, the bush burned with fire, and the bush *was* not consumed.

5. Jos 5:14 And he said, Nay; but *as* captain of the host of the LORD am I now come. And Joshua fell on his face to the earth, and did worship, and said unto him, What saith my lord unto his servant?

6. Jdg 6:22 And when Gideon perceived that he *was* an angel of the LORD, Gideon said, Alas, O Lord GOD! for because I have seen an angel of the LORD face to face.

7. Jdg 13:22 And Manoah said unto his wife, We shall surely die, because we have seen God.

8. 2Ki 19:35 And it came to pass that night, that the angel of the LORD went out, and smote in the camp of the Assyrians an hundred fourscore and five thousand: and when they arose early in the morning, behold, they *were* all dead corpses.

9. Dan 3:25 He answered and said, Lo, I see four men loose, walking in the midst of the fire, and they have no hurt; and the form of the fourth is like the Son of God.

10. Zec 12:8 In that day shall the LORD defend the inhabitants of Jerusalem; and he that is feeble among them at that day shall be as David; and the house of David *shall be* as God, as the angel of the LORD before them.

List of Possible Christ Types in the Old Testament

WHAT FOLLOWS IS A LIST of people and things that were symbolic representations of some of Christ' attributes or that image Christ in some other way. This is probably a partial list of Christ-Types.

1. Adam- Image of God, Sinless/Innocent (well started out as).

2. Abraham- Friend of God, Faithful.

3. Melchizedek- without father/mother, king of righteouness & peace, Immortal.

4. Isaac- The sacrificial son.

5. Noah- Perfect, preacher of righteousness.

6. Moses- Miracle worker, Shepherd, Prophet.

7. David- Loved God with perfect heart, King, Shepherd, Warrior.

8. Joseph- Persecuted though innocent, Deliverer.

9. Joshua- Overcomer, Warrior.

10. Jonah- 3 days and nights in whale (possibly dead).

11. Solomon- Unparalleled wealth and wisdom.

12. Ark- The door to escape God's wrath.

13. Brazen Serpent- was lifted up that whosoever looketh unto it was spared.

14. Job- Perfect yet suffered

Chapter 2: Virtues & Good Fruit

Good Fruit / Christian Attitude

There are many who are so-called "Christian", however the sad reality is, there are very few who actually walk what they profess. While it's true that no one is sinless, saving Christ Jesus. It is also true however, that if one truly has a born again experience by truly believing on the Messiah, then it should follow that their life will show that they are walking with the Lord. Through the lifelong process of sanctification true Christ followers will gradually become more like their heavenly Master. Below are just some of the qualities one should expect a believer in Christ to possess; to keep this section relatively short I'll list just around thirty, along with the supporting and other verses.

Also in order to give the reader an idea of what virtues/topics the remainder of the book covers, I have decided to **bold** all the following examples that I cover in their own section (topic) later on.

1. **Not just loving your friends but also those that hate you.**
2. Not seeking vengeance.
3. **Giving to people who ask for something.**
4. Treating others the way you want to be treated.
5. **Being Merciful.**
6. In order to bear fruit we must abide in Christ.
7. How we respond in tribulation is important as well, we are to glory in it.
8. Abhorring evil but clinging to good.
9. Hard working
10. **Patient under difficult circumstances.**
11. **Giving to the saints.**
12. Hospitable.
13. Empathetic.
14. **Peaceable.**
15. Not self-centered.
16. Not Envious.
17. Not Proud.
18. Rejoices in truth, not in iniquity.

19. **Cheerful in giving, not grudgingly.**
20. Exhibits the fruit of the Spirit (**love, joy, peace,** long suffering, **faith, temperance,** meekness, etc.)
21. Possesses forbearance in love.
22. Can handle **Criticism,** (being submissive to the brethren).
23. Gives cares to the Lord.
24. Content in all circumstances.
25. **Kind to others.**
26. Thankful.
27. Sober.
28. Esteem those that are over them in the Lord very highly.
29. Can rebuke or reprove others.
30. Helping those weaker than themselves.
31. Courteous.
32. Speaks no evil.

Mat 7:17 Even so every good tree bringeth forth good fruit; but a corrupt tree bringeth forth evil fruit.

Mat 7:18 A good tree cannot bring forth evil fruit, neither can a corrupt tree bring forth good fruit.

Luk 6:27 But I say unto you which hear, Love your enemies, do good to them which hate you,

Luk 6:28 Bless them that curse you, and pray for them which despitefully use you.

Luk 6:29 And unto him that smiteth thee on the one cheek offer also the other; and him that taketh away thy cloke forbid not to take thy coat also.

Luk 6:30 Give to every man that asketh of thee; and of him that taketh away thy goods ask them not again.

Luk 6:31 And as ye would that men should do to you, do ye also to them likewise.

Luk 6:35 But love ye your enemies, and do good, and lend, hoping for nothing again; and your reward shall be great, and ye shall be the children of the Highest: for he is kind unto the unthankful and to the evil.

Luk 6:36 Be ye therefore merciful, as your Father also is merciful.

Joh 15:4 Abide in me, and I in you. As the branch cannot bear fruit of itself, except it abide in the vine; no more can ye, except ye abide in me.

Joh 15:5 I am the vine, ye are the branches: He that abideth in me, and I in him, the same bringeth forth much fruit: for without me ye can do nothing.

Rom 5:3 And not only so, but we glory in tribulations also: knowing that tribulation worketh patience;

Rom 5:4 And patience, experience; and experience, hope:

Rom 5:5 And hope maketh not ashamed; because the love of God is shed abroad in our hearts by the Holy Ghost which is given unto us.

Rom 12:9 Let love be without dissimulation. Abhor that which is evil; cleave to that which is good.

Rom 12:10 Be kindly affected one to another with brotherly love; in honour preferring one another;

Rom 12:11 Not slothful in business; fervent in spirit; serving the Lord;

Rom 12:12 Rejoicing in hope; patient in tribulation; continuing instant in prayer;

Rom 12:13 Distributing to the necessity of saints; given to hospitality.

Rom 12:14 Bless them which persecute you: bless, and curse not.

Rom 12:15 Rejoice with them that do rejoice, and weep with them that weep.

Rom 12:16 Be of the same mind one toward another. Mind not high things, but condescend to men of low estate. Be not wise in your own conceits.

Rom 12:17 Recompense to no man evil for evil. Provide things honest in the sight of all men.

Rom 12:18 If it be possible, as much as lieth in you, live peaceably with all men.

Rom 12:19 Dearly beloved, avenge not yourselves, but rather give place unto wrath: for it is written, Vengeance is mine; I will repay, saith the Lord.

Rom 12:20 Therefore if thine enemy hunger, feed him; if he thirst, give him drink: for in so doing thou shalt heap coals of fire on his head.

Rom 12:21 Be not overcome of evil, but overcome evil with good.

Rom 15:1 We then that are strong ought to bear the infirmities of the weak, and not to please ourselves.

Rom 15:2 Let every one of us please his neighbour for his good to edification.

1Co 13:4 Charity suffereth long, and is kind; charity envieth not; charity vaunteth not itself, is not puffed up,

1Co 13:5 Doth not behave itself unseemly, seeketh not her own, is not easily provoked, thinketh no evil;

1Co 13:6 Rejoiceth not in iniquity, but rejoiceth in the truth;

1Co 13:7 Beareth all things, believeth all things, hopeth all things, endureth all things.

2Co 5:7 (For we walk by faith, not by sight:)

2Co 9:7 Every man according as he purposeth in his heart, so let him give; not grudgingly, or of necessity: for God loveth a cheerful giver.

Gal 5:22 But the fruit of the Spirit is love, joy, peace, longsuffering, gentleness, goodness, faith,

Gal 5:23 Meekness, temperance: against such there is no law.

Eph 3:16 That he would grant you, according to the riches of his glory, to be strengthened with might by his Spirit in the inner man;

Eph 3:17 That Christ may dwell in your hearts by faith; that ye, being rooted and grounded in love,

Eph 3:18 May be able to comprehend with all saints what is the breadth, and length, and depth, and height;

Eph 3:19 And to know the love of Christ, which passeth knowledge, that ye might be filled with all the fulness of God.

Eph 4:2 With all lowliness and meekness, with longsuffering, forbearing one another in love;

Eph 4:3 Endeavouring to keep the unity of the Spirit in the bond of peace.

Eph 5:21 Submitting yourselves one to another in the fear of God.

Php 2:3 Let nothing be done through strife or vainglory; but in lowliness of mind let each esteem other better than themselves.

Php 4:4 Rejoice in the Lord alway: and again I say, Rejoice.

Php 4:5 Let your moderation be known unto all men. The Lord is at hand.

Php 4:6 Be careful for nothing; but in every thing by prayer and supplication with thanksgiving let your requests be made known unto God.

Php 4:11 Not that I speak in respect of want: for I have learned, in whatsoever state I am, therewith to be content.

Col 1:10 That ye might walk worthy of the Lord unto all pleasing, being fruitful in every good work, and increasing in the knowledge of God;

Col 1:11 Strengthened with all might, according to his glorious power, unto all patience and longsuffering with joyfulness;

Col 3:12 Put on therefore, as the elect of God, holy and beloved, bowels of mercies, kindness, humbleness of mind, meekness, longsuffering;

Col 3:14 And above all these things *put on* charity, which is the bond of perfectness.

Col 3:15 And let the peace of God rule in your hearts, to the which also ye are called in one body; and be ye thankful.

Col 3:16 Let the word of Christ dwell in you richly in all wisdom; teaching and admonishing one another in psalms and hymns and spiritual songs, singing with grace in your hearts to the Lord.

Col 3:17 And whatsoever ye do in word or deed, *do* all in the name of the Lord Jesus, giving thanks to God and the Father by him.

Col 4:5 Walk in wisdom toward them that are without, redeeming the time.

Col 4:6 Let your speech *be* alway with grace, seasoned with salt, that ye may know how ye ought to answer every man.

1 Th 4:11 And that ye study to be quiet, and to do your own business, and to work with your own hands, as we commanded you;

1 Th 4:12 That ye may walk honestly toward them that are without, and *that* ye may have lack of nothing.

1 Th 5:8 But let us, who are of the day, be sober, putting on the breastplate of faith and love; and for an helmet, the hope of salvation.

1 Th 5:12 And we beseech you, brethren, to know them which labour among you, and are over you in the Lord, and admonish you;

1 Th 5:13 And to esteem them very highly in love for their work's sake. *And* be at peace among yourselves.

1 Th 5:14 Now we exhort you, brethren, warn them that are unruly, comfort the feebleminded, support the weak, be patient toward all *men.*

1 Th 5:15 See that none render evil for evil unto any *man;* but ever follow that which is good, both among yourselves, and to all *men.*

1 Th 5:16 Rejoice evermore.

1Th 5:17 Pray without ceasing.

1Th 5:18 In every thing give thanks: for this is the will of God in Christ Jesus concerning you.

1Th 5:19 Quench not the Spirit.

1Th 5:20 Despise not prophesyings.

1Th 5:21 Prove all things; hold fast that which is good.

1Th 5:22 Abstain from all appearance of evil.

2Ti 4:2 Preach the word; be instant in season, out of season; reprove, rebuke, exhort with all longsuffering and doctrine.

Tit 1:5 For this cause left I thee in Crete, that thou shouldest set in order the things that are wanting, and ordain elders in every city, as I had appointed thee:

Tit 1:6 If any be blameless, the husband of one wife, having faithful children not accused of riot or unruly.

Tit 1:7 For a bishop must be blameless, as the steward of God; not selfwilled, not soon angry, not given to wine, no striker, not given to filthy lucre;

Tit 1:8 But a lover of hospitality, a lover of good men, sober, just, holy, temperate;

Tit 1:9 Holding fast the faithful word as he hath been taught, that he may be able by sound doctrine both to exhort and to convince the gainsayers.

Tit 2:6 Young men likewise exhort to be sober minded.

Tit 2:7 In all things shewing thyself a pattern of good works: in doctrine *shewing* uncorruptness, gravity, sincerity,

Tit 2:8 Sound speech, that cannot be condemned; that he that is of the contrary part may be ashamed, having no evil thing to say of you.

Heb 3:13 But exhort one another daily, while it is called To day; lest any of you be hardened through the deceitfulness of sin.

Jas 3:13 Who is a wise man and endued with knowledge among you? let him shew out of a good conversation his works with meekness of wisdom.

Jas 3:17 But the wisdom that is from above is first pure, then peaceable, gentle, *and* easy to be intreated, full of mercy and good fruits, without partiality, and without hypocrisy.

Jas 4:7 Submit yourselves therefore to God. Resist the devil, and he will flee from you.

Jas 4:8 Draw nigh to God, and he will draw nigh to you. Cleanse your hands, ye sinners; and purify your hearts, ye double minded.

1Pe 1:22 Seeing ye have purified your souls in obeying the truth through the Spirit unto unfeigned love of the brethren, *see that ye* love one another with a pure heart fervently:

1Pe 3:8 Finally, *be ye* all of one mind, having compassion one of another, love as brethren, *be* pitiful, *be* courteous:

1Pe 3:9 Not rendering evil for evil, or railing for railing: but contrariwise blessing; knowing that ye are thereunto called, that ye should inherit a blessing.

1Pe 3:10 For he that will love life, and see good days, let him refrain his tongue from evil, and his lips that they speak no guile:

1Pe 3:11 Let him eschew evil, and do good; let him seek peace, and ensue it.

2Pe 1:5 And beside this, giving all diligence, add to your faith virtue; and to virtue knowledge;

2Pe 1:6 And to knowledge temperance; and to temperance patience; and to patience godliness;

2Pe 1:7 And to godliness brotherly kindness; and to brotherly kindness charity.

2Pe 1:8 For if these things be in you, and abound, they make you that ye shall neither be barren nor unfruitful in the knowledge of our Lord Jesus Christ.

1Jn 2:3 And hereby we do know that we know him, if we keep his commandments.

1Jn 2:4 He that saith, I know him, and keepeth not his commandments, is a liar, and the truth is not in him.

1Jn 2:5 But whoso keepeth his word, in him verily is the love of God perfected: hereby know we that we are in him.

1Jn 2:6 He that saith he abideth in him ought himself also so to walk, even as he walked.

1Jn 3:16 Hereby perceive we the love *of God,* because he laid down his life for us: and we ought to lay down *our* lives for the brethren.

Faith

FAITH IS ONE OF THE most discussed and necessary topics of the bible. That is because without faith we cannot be saved. It is through faith that God imparts his saving grace on us. In other words unbelievers will not inherit the kingdom. Faith is the shield of the Christian's arsenal. It is by faith we walk, not by sight. We must trust God in all circumstances. It is by faith that we trust that God is working all things together for our good. It is by faith that we trust in Jesus' sacrifice on the cross to pay for our sins. Faith is a spiritual gift as well as a biblical command. Their are also different measures of faith as scripture indicates that their is some weak in the faith, as well as Jesus' statement "...O thou of little faith...". So let us be Believers of great faith.

Scripture also warns us that some will depart from the faith, that there are those that deny the faith, as well as those that have made shipwreck of their faith. There are also those that have cast off their first faith, we do not want to be in any of these categories. The bible is clear that faith without works is dead; we want to have living faith. A faith that produces good fruit, we want the Master to say well done, thou good and faithful servant, enter thou into the joy of the Lord.

Anybody can say they have faith, but faith is something that must be exercised. We show our faith by our works. Are we trusting in Jesus to provide for our physical needs or are we trusting in ourselves, our job, our money? What about our health, do we visit the doctor at the slightest headache or take a bunch of medication; or do we rely on the great physician. Are we trusting in God to save us or are we fretting and worried all the time about going to hell or trusting in our own righteousness. Let us take God at his word for he cannot lie and he abideth faithful.

Hebrews 11 is undoubtedly one of the most popular chapters on faith. It gives examples of many of the Old Testament patriarchs and followers of God exhibiting their faith in troublesome and/or uncertain circumstances. Among these is Abraham (concerning his sojourn in a strange land), Abel (concerning his more perfect sacrifice), Sarah (receiving strength to conceive), Noah (building the ark), Enoch (who pleased God and was translated), Isaac and Jacob (blessed their sons by faith), and what about Moses, Samson, Rahab, Gideon, Jephthah, Samuel, David and all the others as well? All these acted in faith and are examples to us as believers.

When we pray we must exercise our faith and not be double minded. For James tells us that those who are double-minded should not expect anything from the Lord. When Jesus was approached in multiple instances throughout the gospels for healing, or deliverance; we see Jesus stating that their faith was what made them whole, or that it saved them (though in reference to salvation, it was the woman of Luke 7 that exercised saving faith). That passage of scripture is particularly moving in my opinion.

Deu 32:20 And he said, I will hide my face from them, I will see what their end *shall be:* for they *are* a very froward generation, children in whom *is* no faith.

Hab 2:4 Behold, his soul *which* is lifted up is not upright in him: but the just shall live by his faith.

Mat 9:22 But Jesus turned him about, and when he saw her, he said, Daughter, be of good comfort; thy faith hath made thee whole. And the woman was made whole from that hour.

Mat 9:29 Then touched he their eyes, saying, According to your faith be it unto you.

Mat 14:31 And immediately Jesus stretched forth *his* hand, and caught him, and said unto him, O thou of little faith, wherefore didst thou doubt?

Mat 21:21 Jesus answered and said unto them, Verily I say unto you, If ye have faith, and doubt not, ye shall not only do this *which is done* to the fig tree, but also if ye shall say unto this mountain, Be thou removed, and be thou cast into the sea; it shall be done.

Mar 4:40 And he said unto them, Why are ye so fearful? how is it that ye have no faith?

Mar 11:22 And Jesus answering saith unto them, Have faith in God.

Luk 5:20 And when he saw their faith, he said unto him, Man, thy sins are forgiven thee.

Luk 7:9 When Jesus heard these things, he marvelled at him, and turned him about, and said unto the people that followed him, I say unto you, I have not found so great faith, no, not in Israel.

Luk 7:50 And he said to the woman, Thy faith hath saved thee; go in peace.

Luk 17:5 And the apostles said unto the Lord, Increase our faith.

Luk 18:8 I tell you that he will avenge them speedily. Nevertheless when the Son of man cometh, shall he find faith on the earth?

Act 3:16 And his name through faith in his name hath made this man strong, whom ye see and know: yea, the faith which is by him hath given him this perfect soundness in the presence of you all.

Act 14:22 Confirming the souls of the disciples, *and* exhorting them to continue in the faith, and that we must through much tribulation enter into the kingdom of God.

Act 20:21 Testifying both to the Jews, and also to the Greeks, repentance toward God, and faith toward our Lord Jesus Christ.

Rom 3:22 Even the righteousness of God *which is* by faith of Jesus Christ unto all and upon all them that believe: for there is no difference:

Rom 3:25 Whom God hath set forth *to be* a propitiation through faith in his blood, to declare his righteousness for the remission of sins that are past, through the forbearance of God;

Rom 3:27 Where *is* boasting then? It is excluded. By what law? of works? Nay: but by the law of faith.

Rom 3:28 Therefore we conclude that a man is justified by faith without the deeds of the law.

Rom 3:30 Seeing *it is* one God, which shall justify the circumcision by faith, and uncircumcision through faith.

Rom 4:5 But to him that worketh not, but believeth on him that justifieth the ungodly, his faith is counted for righteousness.

Rom 4:14 For if they which are of the law *be* heirs, faith is made void, and the promise made of none effect:

Rom 4:16 Therefore *it is* of faith, that *it might be* by grace; to the end the promise might be sure to all the seed; not to that only which is of the law, but to that also which is of the faith of Abraham; who is the father of us all,

Rom 5:1 Therefore being justified by faith, we have peace with God through our Lord Jesus Christ:

Rom 9:32 Wherefore? Because *they sought it* not by faith, but as it were by the works of the law. For they stumbled at that stumblingstone;

Rom 14:1 Him that is weak in the faith receive ye, *but* not to doubtful disputations.

1Co 12:9 To another faith by the same Spirit; to another the gifts of healing by the same Spirit;

1Co 13:2 And though I have *the gift of* prophecy, and understand all mysteries, and all knowledge; and though I have all faith, so that I could remove mountains, and have not charity, I am nothing.

1Co 13:13 And now abideth faith, hope, charity, these three; but the greatest of these *is* charity.

2Co 5:7 (For we walk by faith, not by sight:)

2Co 10:15 Not boasting of things without *our* measure, *that is,* of other men's labours; but having hope, when your faith is increased, that we shall be enlarged by you according to our rule abundantly,

Gal 2:16 Knowing that a man is not justified by the works of the law, but by the faith of Jesus Christ, even we have believed in Jesus Christ, that we might be justified by the faith of Christ, and not by the works of the law: for by the works of the law shall no flesh be justified.

Gal 3:7 Know ye therefore that they which are of faith, the same are the children of Abraham.

Gal_3:8 And the scripture, foreseeing that God would justify the heathen through faith, preached before the gospel unto Abraham, *saying,* In thee shall all nations be blessed.

Gal 3:26 For ye are all the children of God by faith in Christ Jesus.

Eph 6:16 Above all, taking the shield of faith, wherewith ye shall be able to quench all the fiery darts of the wicked.

1Th 1:3 Remembering without ceasing your work of faith, and labour of love, and patience of hope in our Lord Jesus Christ, in the sight of God and our Father;

2Th 3:2 And that we may be delivered from unreasonable and wicked men: for all *men* have not faith.

1Ti 1:5 Now the end of the commandment is charity out of a pure heart, and *of* a good conscience, and *of* faith unfeigned:

1Ti 1:19 Holding faith, and a good conscience; which some having put away concerning faith have made shipwreck:

1Ti 5:12 Having damnation, because they have cast off their first faith.

1Ti 6:10 For the love of money is the root of all evil: which while some coveted after, they have erred from the faith, and pierced themselves through with many sorrows.

1Ti 6:11 But thou, O man of God, flee these things; and follow after righteousness, godliness, faith, love, patience, meekness.

1Ti 6:12 Fight the good fight of faith, lay hold on eternal life, whereunto thou art also called, and hast professed a good profession before many witnesses.

2Ti 4:7 I have fought a good fight, I have finished *my* course, I have kept the faith:

Heb 4:2 For unto us was the gospel preached, as well as unto them: but the word preached did not profit them, not being mixed with faith in them that heard *it.*

Heb 10:22 Let us draw near with a true heart in full assurance of faith, having our hearts sprinkled from an evil conscience, and our bodies washed with pure water.

Heb 10:23 Let us hold fast the profession of *our* faith without wavering; (for he *is* faithful that promised;)

Heb 10:38 Now the just shall live by faith: but if *any man* draw back, my soul shall have no pleasure in him.

See Hebrews Ch. 11 for alot of verses.

Jas 2:14 What *doth it* profit, my brethren, though a man say he hath faith, and have not works? can faith save him?

Jas 2:17 Even so faith, if it hath not works, is dead, being alone.

Jas 2:18 Yea, a man may say, Thou hast faith, and I have works: shew me thy faith without thy works, and I will shew thee my faith by my works.

1Pe 1:7 That the trial of your faith, being much more precious than of gold that perisheth, though it be tried with fire, might be found unto praise and honour and glory at the appearing of Jesus Christ:

1Pe 1:9 Receiving the end of your faith, *even* the salvation of *your* souls.

1Pe 1:21 Who by him do believe in God, that raised him up from the dead, and gave him glory; that your faith and hope might be in God.

1Jn 5:4 For whatsoever is born of God overcometh the world: and this is the victory that overcometh the world, *even* our faith.

Jud 1:3 Beloved, when I gave all diligence to write unto you of the common salvation, it was needful for me to write unto you, and exhort *you* that ye should earnestly contend for the faith which was once delivered unto the saints.

Rev 14:12 Here is the patience of the saints: here *are* they that keep the commandments of God, and the faith of Jesus.

Joy

JOY IS THE FRUIT OF the Spirit; it is not determined by our circumstances as is the case with happiness. Is a distinguishing characteristic of a true believer of Christ. All the worlds pleasures and temptations may bring an element of happiness with them but they are fleeting and can never truly fill the longing of our souls. When one is in a right relationship with their Creator and walking in his will, it will come as no surprise if they were filled with joy. Joy is one of the true treasures of life and I am inclined to believe that it can not be acquired outside of Jesus Christ.

When we look at the world around us and at those who are not yet born again, we can easily see that they lack joy. The lost cuss, complain, get angry easy, suffer from depression, worry, anxiety, etc. They may be happy at times when things are going their way. They may get a raise, their team wins the game, they hit the lotto, get a new girlfriend, or collect some new trinket. However this is temporal happiness, the things of this world never do truly satisfy the soul. I remember back when I was a teen and even into my early 20's I was a huge dragonball fanatic (In case you're wondering dragonball is a Japanese anime that I haven't the desire to go into the depth of what it is here). I used to collect dragonball dvd's, manga, action figures, and cards; but no matter how much I had obtained It didn't bring me joy. Sure I was happy for a little while but of course that sensation fades after a while.

True joy can only come if we are heavenly minded, it cannot be obtained by being obsessed with the things of this world. For the things of this world are temporal and eventually fade away. The only thing that matters in the grand scheme of things is what we did with the life that God gave us. Do we have a relationship with Jesus? Do we talk to him daily (pray), study his word, and are we willing vessels in order to show his love to others; as in letting him live through you.

How can we have true joy if we hurt others, robbing our fellow man, coveting what we don't have, envying others places in life, lusting after our neighbors wives, harboring bitterness, resentment, and unforgiveness over wrongs committed against us. These things destroy our joy and peace, do you want joy? Try being thankful for what you already have, count your blessings. Thank the Lord for your health, finances, car, job, spouse, friends, family, pets, computer, bed, clothes, food, books, house, etc. Ask the Lord for joy. It also helps instead of worrying about your problems; give them to Jesus and instead focus on helping others. Being selfless and helping the needy really is a mood booster. Let God use your body to bless others.

1KI 1:40 AND ALL THE people came up after him, and the people piped with pipes, and rejoiced with great joy, so that the earth rent with the sound of them.

1Ki 8:66 On the eighth day he sent the people away: and they blessed the king, and went unto their tents joyful and glad of heart for all the goodness that the LORD had done for David his servant, and for Israel his people.

1Ch 12:40 Moreover they that were nigh them, even unto Issachar and Zebulun and Naphtali, brought bread on asses, and on camels, and on mules, and on oxen, and meat, meal, cakes of figs, and bunches of raisins, and wine, and oil, and oxen, and sheep abundantly: for there was joy in Israel.

1Ch 15:16 And David spake to the chief of the Levites to appoint their brethren to be the singers with instruments of musick, psalteries and harps and cymbals, sounding, by lifting up the voice with joy.

1Ch 29:9 Then the people rejoiced, for that they offered willingly, because with perfect heart they offered willingly to the LORD: and David the king also rejoiced with great joy.

Ezr 6:16 And the children of Israel, the priests, and the Levites, and the rest of the children of the captivity, kept the dedication of this house of God with joy,

Ezr 6:22 And kept the feast of unleavened bread seven days with joy: for the LORD had made them joyful, and turned the heart of the king of Assyria unto them, to strengthen their hands in the work of the house of God, the God of Israel.

Neh 8:10 Then he said unto them, Go your way, eat the fat, and drink the sweet, and send portions unto them for whom nothing is prepared: for this day is holy unto our Lord: neither be ye sorry; for the joy of the LORD is your strength.

Neh 12:43 Also that day they offered great sacrifices, and rejoiced: for God had made them rejoice with great joy: the wives also and the children rejoiced: so that the joy of Jerusalem was heard even afar off.

Est 9:22 As the days wherein the Jews rested from their enemies, and the month which was turned unto them from sorrow to joy, and from mourning into a good day: that they should make them days of feasting and joy, and of sending portions one to another, and gifts to the poor.

Job 20:5 That the triumphing of the wicked is short, and the joy of the hypocrite but for a moment?

Job 33:26 He shall pray unto God, and he will be favourable unto him: and he shall see his face with joy: for he will render unto man his righteousness.

Job 38:7 When the morning stars sang together, and all the sons of God shouted for joy?

Psa 5:11 But let all those that put their trust in thee rejoice: let them ever shout for joy, because thou defendest them: let them also that love thy name be joyful in thee.

Psa 16:11 Thou wilt shew me the path of life: in thy presence is fulness of joy; at thy right hand there are pleasures for evermore.

Psa 30:5 For his anger endureth but a moment; in his favour is life: weeping may endure for a night, but joy cometh in the morning.

Psa 32:11 Be glad in the LORD, and rejoice, ye righteous: and shout for joy, all ye that are upright in heart.

Psa 51:8 Make me to hear joy and gladness; that the bones which thou hast broken may rejoice.

Psa 67:4 O let the nations be glad and sing for joy: for thou shalt judge the people righteously, and govern the nations upon earth. Selah.

Psa 95:2 Let us come before his presence with thanksgiving, and make a joyful noise unto him with psalms.

Psa 98:4 Make a joyful noise unto the LORD, all the earth: make a loud noise, and rejoice, and sing praise.

Psa 100:1 A Psalm of praise. Make a joyful noise unto the LORD, all ye lands.

Psa 105:43 And he brought forth his people with joy, and his chosen with gladness:

Psa 126:5 They that sow in tears shall reap in joy.

Psa 132:9 Let thy priests be clothed with righteousness; and let thy saints shout for joy.

Psa 137:6 If I do not remember thee, let my tongue cleave to the roof of my mouth; if I prefer not Jerusalem above my chief joy.

Psa 149:2 Let Israel rejoice in him that made him: let the children of Zion be joyful in their King.

Pro 12:20 Deceit is in the heart of them that imagine evil: but to the counsellors of peace is joy.

Pro 14:10 The heart knoweth his own bitterness; and a stranger doth not intermeddle with his joy.

Pro 15:23 A man hath joy by the answer of his mouth: and a word spoken in due season, how good is it!

Pro 17:21 He that begetteth a fool doeth it to his sorrow: and the father of a fool hath no joy.

Pro 23:24 The father of the righteous shall greatly rejoice: and he that begetteth a wise child shall have joy of him.

Ecc 2:26 For God giveth to a man that is good in his sight wisdom, and knowledge, and joy: but to the sinner he giveth travail, to gather and to heap up, that he may give to him that is good before God. This also is vanity and vexation of spirit.

Ecc 7:14 In the day of prosperity be joyful, but in the day of adversity consider: God also hath set the one over against the other, to the end that man should find nothing after him.

Ecc 9:7 Go thy way, eat thy bread with joy, and drink thy wine with a merry heart; for God now accepteth thy works.

Ecc 9:9 Live joyfully with the wife whom thou lovest all the days of the life of thy vanity, which he hath given thee under the sun, all the days of thy vanity: for that is thy portion in this life, and in thy labour which thou takest under the sun.

Isa 9:17 Therefore the Lord shall have no joy in their young men, neither shall have mercy on their fatherless and widows: for every one is an hypocrite and an evildoer, and every mouth speaketh folly. For all this his anger is not turned away, but his hand is stretched out still.

Isa 24:11 There is a crying for wine in the streets; all joy is darkened, the mirth of the land is gone.

Isa 29:19 The meek also shall increase their joy in the LORD, and the poor among men shall rejoice in the Holy One of Israel.

Isa 35:10 And the ransomed of the LORD shall return, and come to Zion with songs and everlasting joy upon their heads: they shall obtain joy and gladness, and sorrow and sighing shall flee away.

Isa 51:3 For the LORD shall comfort Zion: he will comfort all her waste places; and he will make her wilderness like Eden, and her desert like the garden of the LORD; joy and gladness shall be found therein, thanksgiving, and the voice of melody.

Isa 51:11 Therefore the redeemed of the LORD shall return, and come with singing unto Zion; and everlasting joy shall be upon their head: they shall obtain gladness and joy; and sorrow and mourning shall flee away.

Isa 55:12 For ye shall go out with joy, and be led forth with peace: the mountains and the hills shall break forth before you into singing, and all the trees of the field shall clap their hands.

Isa 56:7 Even them will I bring to my holy mountain, and make them joyful in my house of prayer: their burnt offerings and their sacrifices shall be accepted upon mine altar; for mine house shall be called an house of prayer for all people.

Isa 61:10 I will greatly rejoice in the LORD, my soul shall be joyful in my God; for he hath clothed me with the garments of salvation, he hath covered me with the robe of righteousness, as a bridegroom decketh himself with ornaments, and as a bride adorneth herself with her jewels.

Isa 65:19 And I will rejoice in Jerusalem, and joy in my people: and the voice of weeping shall be no more heard in her, nor the voice of crying.

Jer 15:16 Thy words were found, and I did eat them; and thy word was unto me the joy and rejoicing of mine heart: for I am called by thy name, O LORD God of hosts.

Jer 31:13 Then shall the virgin rejoice in the dance, both young men and old together: for I will turn their mourning into joy, and will comfort them, and make them rejoice from their sorrow.

Lam 2:15 All that pass by clap their hands at thee; they hiss and wag their head at the daughter of Jerusalem, saying, Is this the city that men call The perfection of beauty, The joy of the whole earth?

Lam 5:15 The joy of our heart is ceased; our dance is turned into mourning.

Eze 24:25 Also, thou son of man, shall it not be in the day when I take from them their strength, the joy of their glory, the desire of their eyes, and that whereupon they set their minds, their sons and their daughters,

Joe 1:12 The vine is dried up, and the fig tree languisheth; the pomegranate tree, the palm tree also, and the apple tree, even all the trees of the field, are withered: because joy is withered away from the sons of men.

Joe 1:16 Is not the meat cut off before our eyes, yea, joy and gladness from the house of our God?

Hab 3:18 Yet I will rejoice in the LORD, I will joy in the God of my salvation.

Zep 3:17 The LORD thy God in the midst of thee is mighty; he will save, he will rejoice over thee with joy; he will rest in his love, he will joy over thee with singing.

Mat 13:44 Again, the kingdom of heaven is like unto treasure hid in a field; the which when a man hath found, he hideth, and for joy thereof goeth and selleth all that he hath, and buyeth that field.

Mat 25:23 His lord said unto him, Well done, good and faithful servant; thou hast been faithful over a few things, I will make thee ruler over many things: enter thou into the joy of thy lord.

Mat 28:8 And they departed quickly from the sepulchre with fear and great joy; and did run to bring his disciples word.

Luk 1:14 And thou shalt have joy and gladness; and many shall rejoice at his birth.

Luk 6:23 Rejoice ye in that day, and leap for joy: for, behold, your reward is great in heaven: for in the like manner did their fathers unto the prophets.

Luk 8:13 They on the rock are they, which, when they hear, receive the word with joy; and these have no root, which for a while believe, and in time of temptation fall away.

Luk 15:7 I say unto you, that likewise joy shall be in heaven over one sinner that repenteth, more than over ninety and nine just persons, which need no repentance.

Luk 24:52 And they worshipped him, and returned to Jerusalem with great joy:

Joh 3:29 He that hath the bride is the bridegroom: but the friend of the bridegroom, which standeth and heareth him, rejoiceth greatly because of the bridegroom's voice: this my joy therefore is fulfilled.

Joh 15:11 These things have I spoken unto you, that my joy might remain in you, and that your joy might be full.

Joh 16:20 Verily, verily, I say unto you, That ye shall weep and lament, but the world shall rejoice: and ye shall be sorrowful, but your sorrow shall be turned into joy.

Joh 16:21 A woman when she is in travail hath sorrow, because her hour is come: but as soon as she is delivered of the child, she remembereth no more the anguish, for joy that a man is born into the world.

Joh 16:22 And ye now therefore have sorrow: but I will see you again, and your heart shall rejoice, and your joy no man taketh from you.

Joh 16:24 Hitherto have ye asked nothing in my name: ask, and ye shall receive, that your joy may be full.

Act 13:52 And the disciples were filled with joy, and with the Holy Ghost.

Act 15:3 And being brought on their way by the church, they passed through Phenice and Samaria, declaring the conversion of the Gentiles: and they caused great joy unto all the brethren.

Act 20:24 But none of these things move me, neither count I my life dear unto myself, so that I might finish my course with joy, and the ministry, which I have received of the Lord Jesus, to testify the gospel of the grace of God.

Rom 5:11 And not only so, but we also joy in God through our Lord Jesus Christ, by whom we have now received the atonement.

Rom 14:17 For the kingdom of God is not meat and drink; but righteousness, and peace, and joy in the Holy Ghost.

Rom 15:13 Now the God of hope fill you with all joy and peace in believing, that ye may abound in hope, through the power of the Holy Ghost.

2Co 1:24 Not for that we have dominion over your faith, but are helpers of your joy: for by faith ye stand.

Gal 5:22 But the fruit of the Spirit is love, joy, peace, longsuffering, gentleness, goodness, faith,

Php 2:2 Fulfil ye my joy, that ye be likeminded, having the same love, being of one accord, of one mind.

Php 4:1 Therefore, my brethren dearly beloved and longed for, my joy and crown, so stand fast in the Lord, my dearly beloved.

1Th 1:6 And ye became followers of us, and of the Lord, having received the word in much affliction, with joy of the Holy Ghost:

1Th 2:19 For what is our hope, or joy, or crown of rejoicing? Are not even ye in the presence of our Lord Jesus Christ at his coming?

Heb 12:2 Looking unto Jesus the author and finisher of our faith; who for the joy that was set before him endured the cross, despising the shame, and is set down at the right hand of the throne of God.

Heb 13:17 Obey them that have the rule over you, and submit yourselves: for they watch for your souls, as they that must give account, that they may do it with joy, and not with grief: for that is unprofitable for you.

1Pe 1:8 Whom having not seen, ye love; in whom, though now ye see him not, yet believing, ye rejoice with joy unspeakable and full of glory:

1Pe 4:13 But rejoice, inasmuch as ye are partakers of Christ's sufferings; that, when his glory shall be revealed, ye may be glad also with exceeding joy.

3Jn 1:4 I have no greater joy than to hear that my children walk in truth.

Self-Control

SELF-CONTROL IS VITAL as a Christian. For how can we expect to be obedient to the word, if we cannot control our speech and/or actions. As Galatians 5 tells us the Spirit and the flesh are at war, that their desires are opposed to each other. Are you a Christian dear reader? We also read in the same Chapter that those who are Christ's have "...crucified the flesh with the affections and lusts. "

We read in the gospels that in order to be true disciples we must pick up our cross, deny ourselves and follow him. We must lay aside self-government and be led by the Spirit. What I mean by that is that we are not to be self-willed (Titus 1:17, 2 Peter 2:10), as that is a form of Idolatry.

There are many areas our life where we must exercise self-control, I will go ahead a list a few examples.

· What comes out of our mouth when provoked by stressors

· What do we do with our eyes and mind when approached by a beautiful women who is not our spouse

· Resisting the urge to sleep in when you have to go to work

· Avoiding toxic substances such as drugs, and drink alcohol/eat sweets only in moderation

· Resisting the urge to get revenge on someone who has wronged you

---

1SA 15:22 AND SAMUEL said, Hath the LORD *as great* delight in burnt offerings and sacrifices, as in obeying the voice of the LORD? Behold, to obey *is* better than sacrifice, *and* to hearken than the fat of rams.

Pro 25:28 He that *hath* no rule over his own spirit *is like* a city *that is* broken down, *and* without walls.

1Co 9:25 And every man that striveth for the mastery is temperate in all things. Now they *do it* to obtain a corruptible crown; but we an incorruptible.

1Co 13:4 Charity suffereth long, *and* is kind; charity envieth not; charity vaunteth not itself, is not puffed up,

1Co 13:5 Doth not behave itself unseemly, seeketh not her own, is not easily provoked, thinketh no evil;

Gal 5:22 But the fruit of the Spirit is love, joy, peace, longsuffering, gentleness, goodness, faith,

Gal 5:23 Meekness, temperance: against such there is no law.

2Ti 3:3 Without natural affection, trucebreakers, false accusers, incontinent, fierce, despisers of those that are good,

Tit 1:7 For a bishop must be blameless, as the steward of God; not selfwilled, not soon angry, not given to wine, no striker, not given to filthy lucre;

Tit 1:8 But a lover of hospitality, a lover of good men, sober, just, holy, temperate;

Tit 2:2 That the aged men be sober, grave, temperate, sound in faith, in charity, in patience.

Jas 1:12 Blessed *is* the man that endureth temptation: for when he is tried, he shall receive the crown of life, which the Lord hath promised to them that love him.

Jas 1:26 If any man among you seem to be religious, and bridleth not his tongue, but deceiveth his own heart, this man's religion *is* vain.

2Pe 1:6 And to knowledge temperance; and to temperance patience; and to patience godliness;

Love

WHEN IT COMES TO THE topic of Love, I prefer to use Voddie Baucham's definition of Love. Which is "An act of the will accompanied by emotion that leads to action on behalf of it's object." Love is not something you just happen to "fall" into, despite what the culture says. You may have attraction to a girl, but that doesn't mean that you love her. Love doesn't tempt someone to sin. Love wants what's best for someone. We love our Family's, our friends, our children; it doesn't mean we are physically attracted to them.

When someone preaches the gospel (when done right), it is motivated by love of it's audience. It desires for people to come to Jesus to receive salvation. On the other hand people may claim to "love" their partner but if they are in a relationship that violates God's commands (i.e. homosexuality, chambering, adultery, incest, etc), then they are causing that person to stand in opposition to God, therefore not having their best interest at heart.

Christians are commanded to love their neighbors, and yes, even their enemies. The first commandment is the Love the Lord with all our heart, soul, mind, and strength. Husbands are told to love their wives as Christ loves the church. Christian's are to esteem very highly in love those that admonish us. We are to love not in tongue & word, but in deed and truth. We are to give to the poor and needy, and help the widow and the fatherless. The bible is clear, If we love Jesus, we will keep his commands. Love is a fruit of the Spirit, and as such is evidence of someone being a child of God.

There is one kind of love that is to be avoided and that is self-love or better put self-centeredness. Selfish is another way to say it. 2 Timothy 3:2 warns us that in the last days men would be lovers of themselves. There are several and/ or bible verses that warn against this including but not limited to Mat 16:24, Mark 8:34, Luke 9:23, John 12:25). Does this mean that Christians are to be miserable, nope, just look at the fruit of the Spirit in Galatians 5. Selfishness will not bring joy, peace, and true love.

EXO 20:6 AND SHEWING mercy unto thousands of them that love me, and keep my commandments.

Lev 19:34 *But* the stranger that dwelleth with you shall be unto you as one born among you, and thou shalt love him as thyself; for ye were strangers in the land of Egypt: I *am* the LORD your God.

Deu 6:5 And thou shalt love the LORD thy God with all thine heart, and with all thy soul, and with all thy might.

Deu 30:6 And the LORD thy God will circumcise thine heart, and the heart of thy seed, to love the LORD thy God with all thine heart, and with all thy soul, that thou mayest live.

2Sa 1:26 I am distressed for thee, my brother Jonathan: very pleasant hast thou been unto me: thy love to me was wonderful, passing the love of women.

2Ch 19:2 And Jehu the son of Hanani the seer went out to meet him, and said to king Jehoshaphat, Shouldest thou help the ungodly, and love them that hate the LORD? therefore *is* wrath upon thee from before the LORD.

Psa 5:11 But let all those that put their trust in thee rejoice: let them ever shout for joy, because thou defendest them: let them also that love thy name be joyful in thee.

Psa 31:23 O love the LORD, all ye his saints: *for* the LORD preserveth the faithful, and plentifully rewardeth the proud doer.

Psa 70:4 Let all those that seek thee rejoice and be glad in thee: and let such as love thy salvation say continually, Let God be magnified.

Psa 119:159 Consider how I love thy precepts: quicken me, O LORD, according to thy lovingkindness.

Psa 119:165 Great peace have they which love thy law: and nothing shall offend them.

Psa 122:6 Pray for the peace of Jerusalem: they shall prosper that love thee.

Psa 145:20 The LORD preserveth all them that love him: but all the wicked will he destroy.

Pro 8:17 I love them that love me; and those that seek me early shall find me.

Pro 10:12 Hatred stirreth up strifes: but love covereth all sins.

Pro 15:17 Better *is* a dinner of herbs where love is, than a stalled ox and hatred therewith.

Ecc 3:8 A time to love, and a time to hate; a time of war, and a time of peace.

Son 1:15 Behold, thou *art* fair, my love; behold, thou *art* fair; thou *hast* doves' eyes.

Son 2:2 As the lily among thorns, so *is* my love among the daughters.

Son 2:4 He brought me to the banqueting house, and his banner over me *was* love.

Son 2:5 Stay me with flagons, comfort me with apples: for I *am* sick of love.

Son 5:2 I sleep, but my heart waketh: *it is* the voice of my beloved that knocketh, *saying,* Open to me, my sister, my love, my dove, my undefiled: for my head is filled with dew, *and* my locks with the drops of the night.

Son 8:4 I charge you, O daughters of Jerusalem, that ye stir not up, nor awake *my* love, until he please.

Son 8:6 Set me as a seal upon thine heart, as a seal upon thine arm: for love *is* strong as death; jealousy *is* cruel as the grave: the coals thereof *are* coals of fire, *which hath a* most vehement flame.

Son 8:7 Many waters cannot quench love, neither can the floods drown it: if *a* man would give all the substance of his house for love, it would utterly be contemned.

Isa 38:17 Behold, for peace I had great bitterness: but thou hast in love to my soul *delivered it* from the pit of corruption: for thou hast cast all my sins behind thy back.

Isa 63:9 In all their affliction he was afflicted, and the angel of his presence saved them: in his love and in his pity he redeemed them; and he bare them, and carried them all the days of old.

Jer 31:3 The LORD hath appeared of old unto me, *saying,* Yea, I have loved thee with an everlasting love: therefore with lovingkindness have I drawn thee.

Eze 16:8 Now when I passed by thee, and looked upon thee, behold, thy time *was* the time of love; and I spread my skirt over thee, and covered thy nakedness: yea, I sware unto thee, and entered into a covenant with thee, saith the Lord GOD, and thou becamest mine.

Hos 3:1 Then said the LORD unto me, Go yet, love a woman beloved of *her* friend, yet an adulteress, according to the love of the LORD toward the children of Israel, who look to other gods, and love flagons of wine.

Hos 9:15 All their wickedness *is* in Gilgal: for there I hated them: for the wickedness of their doings I will drive them out of mine house, I will love them no more: all their princes *are* revolters.

Mic 6:8 He hath shewed thee, O man, what *is* good; and what doth the LORD require of thee, but to do justly, and to love mercy, and to walk humbly with thy God?

Mat 5:44 But I say unto you, Love your enemies, bless them that curse you, do good to them that hate you, and pray for them which despitefully use you, and persecute you;

Mat_5:46 For if ye love them which love you, what reward have ye? do not even the publicans the same?

Mar 12:30 And thou shalt love the Lord thy God with all thy heart, and with all thy soul, and with all thy mind, and with all thy strength: this *is* the first commandment.

Mar 12:31 And the second *is* like, *namely* this, Thou shalt love thy neighbour as thyself. There is none other commandment greater than these.

Luk 6:27 But I say unto you which hear, Love your enemies, do good to them which hate you,

Joh 13:34 A new commandment I give unto you, That ye love one another; as I have loved you, that ye also love one another.

Joh 13:35 By this shall all *men* know that ye are my disciples, if ye have love one to another.

Joh 14:15 If ye love me, keep my commandments.

Joh 14:21 He that hath my commandments, and keepeth them, he it is that loveth me: and he that loveth me shall be loved of my Father, and I will love him, and will manifest myself to him.

Joh 14:23 Jesus answered and said unto him, If a man love me, he will keep my words: and my Father will love him, and we will come unto him, and make our abode with him.

Joh 15:10 If ye keep my commandments, ye shall abide in my love; even as I have kept my Father's commandments, and abide in his love.

Joh 15:12 This is my commandment, That ye love one another, as I have loved you.

Joh 15:13 Greater love hath no man than this, that a man lay down his life for his friends.

Rom 5:8 But God commendeth his love toward us, in that, while we were yet sinners, Christ died for us.

Rom 8:28 And we know that all things work together for good to them that love God, to them who are the called according to *his* purpose.

Rom 8:35 Who shall separate us from the love of Christ? *shall* tribulation, or distress, or persecution, or famine, or nakedness, or peril, or sword?

Rom 8:39 Nor height, nor depth, nor any other creature, shall be able to separate us from the love of God, which is in Christ Jesus our Lord.

Rom 12:9 *Let* love be without dissimulation. Abhor that which is evil; cleave to that which is good.

Rom 12:10 *Be* kindly affectioned one to another with brotherly love; in honour preferring one another;

1Co 2:9 But as it is written, Eye hath not seen, nor ear heard, neither have entered into the heart of man, the things which God hath prepared for them that love him.

1Co 16:22 If any man love not the Lord Jesus Christ, let him be Anathema Maranatha.

2Co 6:6 By pureness, by knowledge, by longsuffering, by kindness, by the Holy Ghost, by love unfeigned,

Eph 3:17 That Christ may dwell in your hearts by faith; that ye, being rooted and grounded in love,

Eph 3:19 And to know the love of Christ, which passeth knowledge, that ye might be filled with all the fulness of God.

Eph 4:2 With all lowliness and meekness, with longsuffering, forbearing one another in love;

Eph 4:15 But speaking the truth in love, may grow up into him in all things, which is the head, *even* Christ:

1Th 3:12 And the Lord make you to increase and abound in love one toward another, and toward all *men,* even as we *do* toward you:

Heb 6:10 For God *is* not unrighteous to forget your work and labour of love, which ye have shewed toward his name, in that ye have ministered to the saints, and do minister.

Heb 10:24 And let us consider one another to provoke unto love and to good works:

Heb 13:1 Let brotherly love continue.

Jas 1:12 Blessed *is* the man that endureth temptation: for when he is tried, he shall receive the crown of life, which the Lord hath promised to them that love him.

Jas 2:8 If ye fulfil the royal law according to the scripture, Thou shalt love thy neighbour as thyself, ye do well:

1Pe 1:22 Seeing ye have purified your souls in obeying the truth through the Spirit unto unfeigned love of the brethren, *see that ye* love one another with a pure heart fervently:

1Jn 3:14 We know that we have passed from death unto life, because we love the brethren. He that loveth not *his* brother abideth in death.

1Jn 3:16 Hereby perceive we the love *of God,* because he laid down his life for us: and we ought to lay down *our* lives for the brethren.

1Jn 3:17 But whoso hath this world's good, and seeth his brother have need, and shutteth up his bowels *of compassion* from him, how dwelleth the love of God in him?

1Jn 3:18 My little children, let us not love in word, neither in tongue; but in deed and in truth.

See 1 John 4.

Discipline

SO WHAT CAN BE SAID about discipline? Although discipline isn't a joyous occasion, it is necessary to build character. When you are a child, your parents (if they are godly) discipline you; when you are older, and if you are a believer, then it is the Lord who disciplines you. Discipline is necessary because it is important for us to realize that there are consequence to our actions. It is a biblical principle that a man reaps what he sows. Sin has very serious consequences and it is better to endure the chastisement of a loved one that to suffer from a heinous vice.

Hebrews 12 is a useful chapter on this subject; it speaks of the chastisement of the Lord, it goes on to tell us that all are partakers of chastisement (that is, unless ye are bastards). The Lord chastises those whom he loves so that we may be made partakers of his holiness; therefore we are not to faint when God corrects us. Now not all bad things that happens to us are a form of Chastisement, some of it is because of our own poor decisions, and some of it is just part of life. Remember we won't have a problem-free life this side of eternity.

The bible tells us to endure chastening and hardness, it also speaks of Paul bringing his body into subjection (he is one of our examples to follow), though our primary example is Christ. The Christian walk ain't easy, there will be trials, temptations, adversity, and persecution. In order to face these challenges in life we need to be God sufficient, not self sufficient (2 Corinthians 1:3-10). So I encourage my readers as Paul did, so run that ye may obtain the prize.

Job 36:10 He openeth also their ear to discipline, and commandeth that they return from iniquity.

Pro 23:13 Withhold not correction from the child: for *if* thou beatest him with the rod, he shall not die.

Pro 23:14 Thou shalt beat him with the rod, and shalt deliver his soul from hell.

1Co 9:24 Know ye not that they which run in a race run all, but one receiveth the prize? So run, that ye may obtain.

1Co 9:25 And every man that striveth for the mastery is temperate in all things. Now they *do it* to obtain a corruptible crown; but we an incorruptible.

1Co 9:26 I therefore so run, not as uncertainly; so fight I, not as one that beateth the air:

1Co 9:27 But I keep under my body, and bring *it* into subjection: lest that by any means, when I have preached to others, I myself should be a castaway.

Gal 6:9 And let us not be weary in well doing: for in due season we shall reap, if we faint not.

1Ti 3:2 A bishop then must be blameless, the husband of one wife, vigilant, sober, of good behaviour, given to hospitality, apt to teach;

1Ti 3:3 Not given to wine, no striker, not greedy of filthy lucre; but patient, not a brawler, not covetous;

1Ti 3:4 One that ruleth well his own house, having his children in subjection with all gravity;

1Ti 3:5 (For if a man know not how to rule his own house, how shall he take care of the church of God?)

2Ti 2:3 Thou therefore endure hardness, as a good soldier of Jesus Christ.

Heb 12:7 If ye endure chastening, God dealeth with you as with sons; for what son is he whom the father chasteneth not?

Jas 1:26 If any man among you seem to be religious, and bridleth not his tongue, but deceiveth his own heart, this man's religion *is* vain.

Patience

PATIENCE, THIS ATTRIBUTE can be more easily said than done for sure. Sometimes in life there are things we are wanting to happen, and it seems like it's taking forever; this can be a job promotion, or it's meeting your future spouse, maybe it's a cure for some illness, or maybe it's for a house, land, friends, or a church. Whatever the situation may be, it is important to wait on God's timing. Sometimes we must put in effort on our part, such as searching for a spouse, or church, or doing our part to eat right or look for land.

Websters Revised Unabridged Dictionary 1913 defines patience as the following: "...1. The state or quality of being patient; the power of suffering with fortitude; uncomplaining endurance of evils or wrongs, as toil, pain, poverty, insult, oppression, calamity, etc...2. The act or power of calmly or contentedly waiting for something due or hoped for; forbearance..."

I will personally admit, I struggle with this virtue, I lose my temper quite easily, and it is unbecoming of a Christian. Some general examples of losing patience include but not limited too, getting road rage, losing your temper when something is spilt or knocked over by a child or animal, verbally abusing someone when they don't do what you ask, cussing when stressed out at work, freaking out because of forgetting something, etc. Patience is one of those inner workings of the Christians life that is just as vital if not more so, than the outer appearance of righteousness than some portray to the world.

Psa 40:1 To the chief Musician, A Psalm of David. I waited patiently for the LORD; and he inclined unto me, and heard my cry.

Psa 37:7 Rest in the LORD, and wait patiently for him: fret not thyself because of him who prospereth in his way, because of the man who bringeth wicked devices to pass.

Ecc 7:8 Better is the end of a thing than the beginning thereof: and the patient in spirit is better than the proud in spirit.

Mat 18:26 The servant therefore fell down, and worshipped him, saying, Lord, have patience with me, and I will pay thee all.

Mat 18:29 And his fellowservant fell down at his feet, and besought him, saying, Have patience with me, and I will pay thee all.

Luk 8:15 But that on the good ground are they, which in an honest and good heart, having heard the word, keep it, and bring forth fruit with patience.

Luk 21:19 In your patience possess ye your souls.

Act 26:3 Especially because I know thee to be expert in all customs and questions which are among the Jews: wherefore I beseech thee to hear me patiently.

Rom 2:7 To them who by patient continuance in well doing seek for glory and honour and immortality, eternal life:

Rom 5:3 And not only so, but we glory in tribulations also: knowing that tribulation worketh patience;

Rom 5:4 And patience, experience; and experience, hope:

Rom 8:25 But if we hope for that we see not, then do we with patience wait for it.

Rom 12:12 Rejoicing in hope; patient in tribulation; continuing instant in prayer;

Rom 15:4 For whatsoever things were written aforetime were written for our learning, that we through patience and comfort of the scriptures might have hope.

Rom 15:5 Now the God of patience and consolation grant you to be likeminded one toward another according to Christ Jesus:

2Co 6:4 But in all things approving ourselves as the ministers of God, in much patience, in afflictions, in necessities, in distresses,

2Co 12:12 Truly the signs of an apostle were wrought among you in all patience, in signs, and wonders, and mighty deeds.

Col 1:11 Strengthened with all might, according to his glorious power, unto all patience and longsuffering with joyfulness;

1Th 1:3 Remembering without ceasing your work of faith, and labour of love, and patience of hope in our Lord Jesus Christ, in the sight of God and our Father;

1Th 5:14 Now we exhort you, brethren, warn them that are unruly, comfort the feebleminded, support the weak, be patient toward all men.

2Th 1:4 So that we ourselves glory in you in the churches of God for your patience and faith in all your persecutions and tribulations that ye endure:

2Th 3:5 And the Lord direct your hearts into the love of God, and into the patient waiting for Christ.

1Ti 3:3 Not given to wine, no striker, not greedy of filthy lucre; but patient, not a brawler, not covetous;

1Ti 6:11 But thou, O man of God, flee these things; and follow after righteousness, godliness, faith, love, patience, meekness.

2Ti 2:24 And the servant of the Lord must not strive; but be gentle unto all men, apt to teach, patient,

2Ti 3:10 But thou hast fully known my doctrine, manner of life, purpose, faith, longsuffering, charity, patience,

Tit 2:2 That the aged men be sober, grave, temperate, sound in faith, in charity, in patience.

Heb 6:12 That ye be not slothful, but followers of them who through faith and patience inherit the promises.

Heb 6:15 And so, after he had patiently endured, he obtained the promise.

Heb 10:36 For ye have need of patience, that, after ye have done the will of God, ye might receive the promise.

Heb 12:1 Wherefore seeing we also are compassed about with so great a cloud of witnesses, let us lay aside every weight, and the sin which doth so easily beset us, and let us run with patience the race that is set before us,

Jas 1:3 Knowing this, that the trying of your faith worketh patience.

Jas 1:4 But let patience have her perfect work, that ye may be perfect and entire, wanting nothing.

Jas 5:7 Be patient therefore, brethren, unto the coming of the Lord. Behold, the husbandman waiteth for the precious fruit of the earth, and hath long patience for it, until he receive the early and latter rain.

Jas 5:8 Be ye also patient; stablish your hearts: for the coming of the Lord draweth nigh.

Jas 5:10 Take, my brethren, the prophets, who have spoken in the name of the Lord, for an example of suffering affliction, and of patience.

Jas 5:11 Behold, we count them happy which endure. Ye have heard of the patience of Job, and have seen the end of the Lord; that the Lord is very pitiful, and of tender mercy.

1Pe 2:20 For what glory is it, if, when ye be buffeted for your faults, ye shall take it patiently? but if, when ye do well, and suffer for it, ye take it patiently, this is acceptable with God.

2Pe 1:6 And to knowledge temperance; and to temperance patience; and to patience godliness;

Rev 1:9 I John, who also am your brother, and companion in tribulation, and in the kingdom and patience of Jesus Christ, was in the isle that is called Patmos, for the word of God, and for the testimony of Jesus Christ.

Rev 2:2 I know thy works, and thy labour, and thy patience, and how thou canst not bear them which are evil: and thou hast tried them which say they are apostles, and are not, and hast found them liars:

Rev 2:3 And hast borne, and hast patience, and for my name's sake hast laboured, and hast not fainted.

Rev 2:19 I know thy works, and charity, and service, and faith, and thy patience, and thy works; and the last to be more than the first.

Rev 3:10 Because thou hast kept the word of my patience, I also will keep thee from the hour of temptation, which shall come upon all the world, to try them that dwell upon the earth.

Rev 13:10 He that leadeth into captivity shall go into captivity: he that killeth with the sword must be killed with the sword. Here is the patience and the faith of the saints.

Rev 14:12 Here is the patience of the saints: here are they that keep the commandments of God, and the faith of Jesus.

Charity

CHARITY IS ONE BIBLICAL command that is repeated in several instances of scripture, particularly the New Testament. So what is Charity? The best place to go for a definition of Charity is 1 Corinthians 13. The first few verses of this chapter stress the essentially of Charity, while the next several verses go on to describe the qualities one must possess in order to be considered charitable.

The Scriptures place a heavy emphasis on the importance of charity, it would seem *(at least to this author)* that one cannot inherit the kingdom without it. The bible says that even if one had all knowledge and faith but not charity, then they would be nothing. Even if they gave away all their goods and sacrificed their life, it would be profitless without charity. Much of charity has to do with the mind, the passages in 1 Corinthians 13 speaks of thought crimes or iniquity, such as envy, pride, selfishness, and a quick temper. This shows that if one professes faith in Christ then these are some of the issues we need to get the victory over, through God's help of course. I would assume that for most people what comes to mind when the word charity is spoken are things like donations, soup kitchens, food pantries, clothing giveaways and things of that sort. But as I said before what we find in 1st Corinthians 13 is that the focus is primarily on our character or how we think/behave. Although there is a phrase in there that indicates a concern for others "seeketh not her known".

It just so happens that I have a little sister who's name is Charice, which is Filipino for charity. Many modern bible versions translate the word charity as love in 1st Corinthians 12. There are three kinds of Greek words for love. There is Agape love which is of the self sacrificial variety, then there is Philia love that is the friendly and brotherly type; I believe this is where the city Philadelphia got it's name, and of coarse there is the Eros love, which is the Erotic, sensual love.

1Co 8:1 Now as touching things offered unto idols, we know that we all have knowledge. Knowledge puffeth up, but charity edifieth.

1Co 13:1 Though I speak with the tongues of men and of angels, and have not charity, I am become as sounding brass, or a tinkling cymbal.

1Co 13:2 And though I have the gift of prophecy, and understand all mysteries, and all knowledge; and though I have all faith, so that I could remove mountains, and have not charity, I am nothing.

1Co 13:3 And though I bestow all my goods to feed the poor, and though I give my body to be burned, and have not charity, it profiteth me nothing.

1Co 13:4 Charity suffereth long, and is kind; charity envieth not; charity vaunteth not itself, is not puffed up,

1Co 13:5 Doth not behave itself unseemly, seeketh not her own, is not easily provoked, thinketh no evil;

1Co 13:6 Rejoiceth not in iniquity, but rejoiceth in the truth;

1Co 13:7 Beareth all things, believeth all things, hopeth all things, endureth all things.

1Co 13:8 Charity never faileth: but whether there be prophecies, they shall fail; whether there be tongues, they shall cease; whether there be knowledge, it shall vanish away.

1Co 13:13 And now abideth faith, hope, charity, these three; but the greatest of these is charity.

1Co 14:1 Follow after charity, and desire spiritual gifts, but rather that ye may prophesy.

1Co 16:14 Let all your things be done with charity.

Col 3:14 And above all these things put on charity, which is the bond of perfectness.

1Th 3:6 But now when Timotheus came from you unto us, and brought us good tidings of your faith and charity, and that ye have good remembrance of us always, desiring greatly to see us, as we also to see you:

2Th 1:3 We are bound to thank God always for you, brethren, as it is meet, because that your faith groweth exceedingly, and the charity of every one of you all toward each other aboundeth;

1Ti 1:5 Now the end of the commandment is charity out of a pure heart, and of a good conscience, and of faith unfeigned:

1Ti 2:15 Notwithstanding she shall be saved in childbearing, if they continue in faith and charity and holiness with sobriety.

1Ti 4:12 Let no man despise thy youth; but be thou an example of the believers, in word, in conversation, in charity, in spirit, in faith, in purity.

2Ti 2:22 Flee also youthful lusts: but follow righteousness, faith, charity, peace, with them that call on the Lord out of a pure heart.

2Ti 3:10 But thou hast fully known my doctrine, manner of life, purpose, faith, longsuffering, charity, patience,

Tit 2:2 That the aged men be sober, grave, temperate, sound in faith, in charity, in patience.

1Pe 4:8 And above all things have fervent charity among yourselves: for charity shall cover the multitude of sins.

1Pe 5:14 Greet ye one another with a kiss of charity. Peace be with you all that are in Christ Jesus. Amen.

2Pe 1:7 And to godliness brotherly kindness; and to brotherly kindness charity.

3Jn 1:6 Which have borne witness of thy charity before the church: whom if thou bring forward on their journey after a godly sort, thou shalt do well:

Jud 1:12 These are spots in your feasts of charity, when they feast with you, feeding themselves without fear: clouds they are without water, carried about of winds; trees whose fruit withereth, without fruit, twice dead, plucked up by the roots;

Rev 2:19 I know thy works, and charity, and service, and faith, and thy patience, and thy works; and the last to be more than the first.

Kindness

A QUOTE FROM WEBSTERS Revised Unabridged Dictionary 1913 on the definition of kind: "...3. Showing tenderness or goodness; disposed to do good and confer happiness; averse to hurting or paining; benevolent; benignant; gracious.

...4. Proceeding from, or characterized by, goodness, gentleness, or benevolence; as, a kind act. "Manners so kind, yet stately..."

Kindness is not to be confused with niceness. Niceness can be defined as pleasing or agreeable, which isn't always biblical, depending on the circumstances. The apostle Paul states in Galatians 1:10 "Gal_1:10 For do I now persuade men, or God? or do I seek to please men? for if I yet pleased men, I should not be the servant of Christ." but in he writes, 1 Corinthians 10:33 "1Co_10:33 Even as I please all *men* in all *things,* not seeking mine own profit, but the *profit* of many, that they may be saved. This apparent contradiction can be cleared up quite easily when we understand the difference between nice and kind. While kindness always has someones best interest at heart, niceness is careful not to offend. When people oppose themselves by sinning, we are to be kind by reproving them; this is spiritual benevolence, and this is why being nice isn't always biblical, because it agrees with the sinner (or at the very least won't speak up), while they engage in sin.

GEN 24:12 AND HE SAID, O LORD God of my master Abraham, I pray thee, send me good speed this day, and shew kindness unto my master Abraham.

Gen 24:49 And now if ye will deal kindly and truly with my master, tell me: and if not, tell me; that I may turn to the right hand, or to the left.

Gen 34:3 And his soul clave unto Dinah the daughter of Jacob, and he loved the damsel, and spake kindly unto the damsel.

Gen 40:14 But think on me when it shall be well with thee, and shew kindness, I pray thee, unto me, and make mention of me unto Pharaoh, and bring me out of this house:

Gen 47:29 And the time drew nigh that Israel must die: and he called his son Joseph, and said unto him, If now I have found grace in thy sight, put, I pray thee, thy hand under my thigh, and deal kindly and truly with me; bury me not, I pray thee, in Egypt:

Gen 50:21 Now therefore fear ye not: I will nourish you, and your little ones. And he comforted them, and spake kindly unto them.

Jos 2:14 And the men answered her, Our life for yours, if ye utter not this our business. And it shall be, when the LORD hath given us the land, that we will deal kindly and truly with thee.

Rth 1:8 And Naomi said unto her two daughters in law, Go, return each to her mother's house: the LORD deal kindly with you, as ye have dealt with the dead, and with me.

1Sa 15:6 And Saul said unto the Kenites, Go, depart, get you down from among the Amalekites, lest I destroy you with them: for ye shewed kindness to all the children of Israel, when they came up out of Egypt. So the Kenites departed from among the Amalekites.

1Sa 20:8 Therefore thou shalt deal kindly with thy servant; for thou hast brought thy servant into a covenant of the LORD with thee: notwithstanding, if there be in me iniquity, slay me thyself; for why shouldest thou bring me to thy father?

2Sa 2:5 And David sent messengers unto the men of Jabeshgilead, and said unto them, Blessed be ye of the LORD, that ye have shewed this kindness unto your lord, even unto Saul, and have buried him.

2Sa 2:6 And now the LORD shew kindness and truth unto you: and I also will requite you this kindness, because ye have done this thing.

2Ki 25:28 And he spake kindly to him, and set his throne above the throne of the kings that were with him in Babylon;

1Ch 19:2 And David said, I will shew kindness unto Hanun the son of Nahash, because his father shewed kindness to me. And David sent messengers to comfort him concerning his father. So the servants of David came into the land of the children of Ammon to Hanun, to comfort him.

Neh 9:17 And refused to obey, neither were mindful of thy wonders that thou didst among them; but hardened their necks, and in their rebellion appointed a captain to return to their bondage: but thou art a God ready to pardon, gracious and merciful, slow to anger, and of great kindness, and forsookest them not.

Est 2:9 And the maiden pleased him, and she obtained kindness of him; and he speedily gave her her things for purification, with such things as belonged to her, and seven maidens, which were meet to be given her, out of the king's house: and he preferred her and her maids unto the best place of the house of the women.

Psa 119:76 Let, I pray thee, thy merciful kindness be for my comfort, according to thy word unto thy servant.

Psa 141:5 Let the righteous smite me; it shall be a kindness: and let him reprove me; it shall be an excellent oil, which shall not break my head: for yet my prayer also shall be in their calamities.

Pro 19:22 The desire of a man is his kindness: and a poor man is better than a liar.

Pro 31:26 She openeth her mouth with wisdom; and in her tongue is the law of kindness.

Isa 54:8 In a little wrath I hid my face from thee for a moment; but with everlasting kindness will I have mercy on thee, saith the LORD thy Redeemer.

Isa 54:10 For the mountains shall depart, and the hills be removed; but my kindness shall not depart from thee, neither shall the covenant of my peace be removed, saith the LORD that hath mercy on thee.

Jer 2:2 Go and cry in the ears of Jerusalem, saying, Thus saith the LORD; I remember thee, the kindness of thy youth, the love of thine espousals, when thou wentest after me in the wilderness, in a land that was not sown.

Jer 52:32 And spake kindly unto him, and set his throne above the throne of the kings that were with him in Babylon,

Joe 2:13 And rend your heart, and not your garments, and turn unto the LORD your God: for he is gracious and merciful, slow to anger, and of great kindness, and repenteth him of the evil.

Jon 4:2 And he prayed unto the LORD, and said, I pray thee, O LORD, was not this my saying, when I was yet in my country? Therefore I fled before unto Tarshish: for I knew that thou art a gracious God, and merciful, slow to anger, and of great kindness, and repentest thee of the evil.

Act 28:2 And the barbarous people shewed us no little kindness: for they kindled a fire, and received us every one, because of the present rain, and because of the cold.

Rom 12:10 Be kindly affectioned one to another with brotherly love; in honour preferring one another;

2Co 6:6 By pureness, by knowledge, by longsuffering, by kindness, by the Holy Ghost, by love unfeigned,

Eph 2:7 That in the ages to come he might shew the exceeding riches of his grace in his kindness toward us through Christ Jesus.

Col 3:12 Put on therefore, as the elect of God, holy and beloved, bowels of mercies, kindness, humbleness of mind, meekness, longsuffering;

Tit 3:4 But after that the kindness and love of God our Saviour toward man appeared,

2Pe 1:7 And to godliness brotherly kindness; and to brotherly kindness charity.

Prayer

THE BIBLE HAS MUCH to say about prayer, as prayer is one of the greatest tools in a Christian's arsenal. Prayer is so important in-fact the bible tells us to pray without ceasing. If you neglect prayer, your spiritual life will suffer. Jesus warns us to not pray to be seen of men, otherwise we'll have no reward of our Heavenly Father. It is important to go to the secret place with our heavenly Father and not just pray when we are out and about; this is because it can be difficult to hear his voice when we are surrounded by noises, and distracted by all the goings-on of the world around us.

We are also not to use vain repetitions when we pray, also it essential that we seek God's will when we pray and not to pray for selfish motives (1John 5, James 4). God knows what is best and he can see the big picture, always keep this in mind when you think your prayers aren't being heard or answered the way that you expect. We must also remember that if there is some secret sin that we are aware of and won't let go, then we can expect God to not listen to our prayers (Psa 66, John 9), God doesn't compromise his righteous standards. Two other things that could block / and /or hinder our prayers is if we have doubt when we pray or if we are mistreating our wife (James 1, Mal 3, 1 Pet 3).

Much can be said about prayer and undoubtedly hundreds of verses could be referenced in this topic, but for this book we won't be covering nearly that many verses. The following are five ways we can pray; followed by the normal-sized list of verses starting from the earlier books to near the ending pages of scripture.

1. Praise

Psa 100:4 Enter into his gates with thanksgiving, and into his courts with praise: be thankful unto him, and bless his name.

2. Thanksgiving

Psa 107:22 And let them sacrifice the sacrifices of thanksgiving, and declare his works with rejoicing.

3. Repentance

Pro 28:13 He that covereth his sins shall not prosper: but whoso confesseth and forsaketh them shall have mercy.

1Jn 1:9 If we confess our sins, he is faithful and just to forgive us our sins, and to cleanse us from all unrighteousness.

4. Intercessions

1Ti 2:1 I exhort therefore, that, first of all, supplications, prayers, intercessions, and giving of thanks, be made for all men;

5. Requests

1Ki 3:9 Give therefore thy servant an understanding heart to judge thy people, that I may discern between good and bad: for who is able to judge this thy so great a people?

1Ki 8:29 That thine eyes may be open toward this house night and day, *even* toward the place of which thou hast said, My name shall be there: that thou mayest hearken unto the prayer which thy servant shall make toward this place.

Psa 66:18 If I regard iniquity in my heart, the Lord will not hear *me:*

Psa 102:17 He will regard the prayer of the destitute, and not despise their prayer.

Pro 15:8 The sacrifice of the wicked *is* an abomination to the LORD: but the prayer of the upright *is* his delight.

Pro 15:29 The LORD *is* far from the wicked: but he heareth the prayer of the righteous.

Pro 21:13 Whoso stoppeth his ears at the cry of the poor, he also shall cry himself, but shall not be heard.

Pro 28:9 He that turneth away his ear from hearing the law, even his prayer *shall be* abomination.

Isa 56:7 Even them will I bring to my holy mountain, and make them joyful in my house of prayer: their burnt offerings and their sacrifices *shall be* accepted upon mine altar; for mine house shall be called an house of prayer for all people.

Isa 59:1 Behold, the LORD'S hand is not shortened, that it cannot save; neither his ear heavy, that it cannot hear:

Isa 59:2 But your iniquities have separated between you and your God, and your sins have hid *his* face from you, that he will not hear.

Mal 2:13 And this have ye done again, covering the altar of the LORD with tears, with weeping, and with crying out, insomuch that he regardeth not the offering any more, or receiveth *it* with good will at your hand.

Mal 2:14 Yet ye say, Wherefore? Because the LORD hath been witness between thee and the wife of thy youth, against whom thou hast dealt treacherously: yet *is* she thy companion, and the wife of thy covenant.

Mat 6:5 And when thou prayest, thou shalt not be as the hypocrites *are:* for they love to pray standing in the synagogues and in the corners of the streets, that they may be seen of men. Verily I say unto you, They have their reward.

Mat 6:6 But thou, when thou prayest, enter into thy closet, and when thou hast shut thy door, pray to thy Father which is in secret; and thy Father which seeth in secret shall reward thee openly.

Mat 6:7 But when ye pray, use not vain repetitions, as the heathen *do:* for they think that they shall be heard for their much speaking.

Mat 6:8 Be not ye therefore like unto them: for your Father knoweth what things ye have need of, before ye ask him.

Mat 6:9 After this manner therefore pray ye: Our Father which art in heaven, Hallowed be thy name.

Mat 6:10 Thy kingdom come. Thy will be done in earth, as *it is* in heaven.

Mat 6:11 Give us this day our daily bread.

Mat 6:12 And forgive us our debts, as we forgive our debtors.

Mat 6:13 And lead us not into temptation, but deliver us from evil: For thine is the kingdom, and the power, and the glory, for ever. Amen.

Mat 18:19 Again I say unto you, That if two of you shall agree on earth as touching any thing that they shall ask, it shall be done for them of my Father which is in heaven.

Mar 11:23 For verily I say unto you, That whosoever shall say unto this mountain, Be thou removed, and be thou cast into the sea; and shall not doubt in his heart, but shall believe that those things which he saith shall come to pass; he shall have whatsoever he saith.

Joh 9:31 Now we know that God heareth not sinners: but if any man be a worshipper of God, and doeth his will, him he heareth.

Joh 14:13 And whatsoever ye shall ask in my name, that will I do, that the Father may be glorified in the Son.

Joh 14:14 If ye shall ask any thing in my name, I will do *it*.

Eph 6:18 Praying always with all prayer and supplication in the Spirit, and watching thereunto with all perseverance and supplication for all saints;

Php 4:6 Be careful for nothing; but in every thing by prayer and supplication with thanksgiving let your requests be made known unto God.

Col 4:2 Continue in prayer, and watch in the same with thanksgiving;

1Ti 4:5 For it is sanctified by the word of God and prayer.

Jas 4:3 Ye ask, and receive not, because ye ask amiss, that ye may consume *it* upon your lusts.

Jas 5:15 And the prayer of faith shall save the sick, and the Lord shall raise him up; and if he have committed sins, they shall be forgiven him.

Jas 5:16 Confess *your* faults one to another, and pray one for another, that ye may be healed. The effectual fervent prayer of a righteous man availeth much.

Jas 5:17 Elias was a man subject to like passions as we are, and he prayed earnestly that it might not rain: and it rained not on the earth by the space of three years and six months.

Jas 5:18 And he prayed again, and the heaven gave rain, and the earth brought forth her fruit.

1Pe 3:7 Likewise, ye husbands, dwell with *them* according to knowledge, giving honour unto the wife, as unto the weaker vessel, and as being heirs together of the grace of life; that your prayers be not hindered.

1Pe 4:7 But the end of all things is at hand: be ye therefore sober, and watch unto prayer.

1Jn 3:22 And whatsoever we ask, we receive of him, because we keep his commandments, and do those things that are pleasing in his sight.

1Jn 5:14 And this is the confidence that we have in him, that, if we ask any thing according to his will, he heareth us:

Jud 1:20 But ye, beloved, building up yourselves on your most holy faith, praying in the Holy Ghost,

Rev 5:8 And when he had taken the book, the four beasts and four *and* twenty elders fell down before the Lamb, having every one of them harps, and golden vials full of odours, which are the prayers of saints.

Giving

THE BIBLE HAS QUITE a lot to say about giving. It instructs us not to turn people away who ask from us. That if we neglect the poor, we also will not be heard. That if we are wealthy and hoard our goods, but do not help the poor, we can expect sore punishment from the almighty. That we are to do our alms in secret, and not brag about them; for if we boast of them, that is to do it for the praise of men, we can not expect to receive a reward from our heavenly Father.

We see this in corporations especially. Big business are frequently bragging or proclaiming how much money they are giving to charitable causes. Sure these organizations donate tens of thousands of dollars or even hundreds of thousands or millions even to help the needy, but if they are sounding a trumpet (so to speak) to be seen of men, then what reward do we expect them to get from God?

We also are to give cheerfully, and not of necessity. Also the more we sow, the more we shall reap. We are not to give to the rich but rather there should be an equality between the believers; those that have an abundance should help the needy. All these valuable lessons about giving are set before us to make us more like Christ Jesus, for he is generous to all.

HERE ARE A FEW SUGGESTIONS on how one can be generous:

- **Donate to a blessing box**

- **Donate used clothes you no longer need or better yet buy new clothes for the poor**

- **Support a ministry that is preaching oversees or that has a YouTube teaching series.**

- **Give to those people who hold cardboard sign (best to do food or clothes though).**

· **Volunteer time to a good cause**

· **Financially give to a disadvantaged Christian in need**

Pro 3:28 Say not unto thy neighbour, Go, and come again, and to morrow I will give; when thou hast it by thee.

Pro 21:13 Whoso stoppeth his ears at the cry of the poor, he also shall cry himself, but shall not be heard.

Pro 22:16 He that oppresseth the poor to increase his *riches, and* he that giveth to the rich, *shall* surely *come* to want.

Mat 5:42 Give to him that asketh thee, and from him that would borrow of thee turn not thou away.

Luk 11:11 If a son shall ask bread of any of you that is a father, will he give him a stone? or if *he ask* a fish, will he for a fish give him a serpent?

Luk 11:12 Or if he shall ask an egg, will he offer him a scorpion?

Luk 11:13 If ye then, being evil, know how to give good gifts unto your children: how much more shall *your* heavenly Father give the Holy Spirit to them that ask him?

Luk 12:16 And he spake a parable unto them, saying, The ground of a certain rich man brought forth plentifully:

Luk 12:17 And he thought within himself, saying, What shall I do, because I have no room where to bestow my fruits?

Luk 12:18 And he said, This will I do: I will pull down my barns, and build greater; and there will I bestow all my fruits and my goods.

Luk 12:19 And I will say to my soul, Soul, thou hast much goods laid up for many years; take thine ease, eat, drink, *and* be merry.

Luk 12:20 But God said unto him, *Thou* fool, this night thy soul shall be required of thee: then whose shall those things be, which thou hast provided?

Luk 12:21 So *is* he that layeth up treasure for himself, and is not rich toward God.

Luk 21:1 And he looked up, and saw the rich men casting their gifts into the treasury.

Luk 21:2 And he saw also a certain poor widow casting in thither two mites.

Luk 21:3 And he said, Of a truth I say unto you, that this poor widow hath cast in more than they all:

Luk 21:4 For all these have of their abundance cast in unto the offerings of God: but she of her penury hath cast in all the living that she had.

Act 20:35 I have shewed you all things, how that so labouring ye ought to support the weak, and to remember the words of the Lord Jesus, how he said, It is more blessed to give than to receive.

2Co 8:12 For if there be first a willing mind, *it is* accepted according to that a man hath, *and* not according to that he hath not.

2Co 8:13 For *I mean* not that other men be eased, and ye burdened:

2Co 8:14 But by an equality, *that* now at this time your abundance *may be a supply* for their want, that their abundance also may be *a supply* for your want: that there may be equality:

2Co 8:15 As it is written, He that *had gathered* much had nothing over; and he that *had gathered* little had no lack.

2Co 9:6 But this *I say,* He which soweth sparingly shall reap also sparingly; and he which soweth bountifully shall reap also bountifully.

2Co 9:7 Every man according as he purposeth in his heart, *so let him give;* not grudgingly, or of necessity: for God loveth a cheerful giver.

Jas 2:15 If a brother or sister be naked, and destitute of daily food,

Jas 2:16 And one of you say unto them, Depart in peace, be *ye* warmed and filled; notwithstanding ye give them not those things which are needful to the body; what *doth it* profit?

Jas 2:17 Even so faith, if it hath not works, is dead, being alone.

Forgiveness

THROUGHOUT THIS LIFE it is almost certain that we will experience hurt, betrayal, rejection, verbal abuse, fraud, or some other type of evil by someone we love, whether it be a family member, friend or acquaintance. This may also be the case in such instances of our enemies. In any case, no matter who it is that has done us wrong, the scripture is clear that we must forgive other if we expects God to forgive us. I mean think about it, we have sinned against God far more times than others have sinned against us ; whether we realize it or not. Deep down we know in our heart that the perfect benevolent Creator wants us to shew mercy on those that have wronged us, and of course; It is the blood of Christ that washes us clean from our sin and grants God's pardon.

Sometimes forgiving others who have wronged us is much easier said than done (especially if it was a very egregious offense, or an offense that happens continually). There is a common saying that unforgiveness is like eating poison and expecting the other person to die. By harboring bitterness and grudges we are doing far more damage to ourselves than to the other person. Scripture says give no place to the devil, therefore we should cast off hatred, lest Satan should get an advantage over us. Yes we must forgive as scripture is quite clear that hatred is a work of the flesh (which forbids entry to the kingdom), and that those that hate their brother are murderers (Gal 5:19-21, 1 John 3:15).

PSA 86:5 FOR THOU, Lord, *art* good, and ready to forgive; and plenteous in mercy unto all them that call upon thee.

Jer 31:34 And they shall teach no more every man his neighbour, and every man his brother, saying, Know the LORD: for they shall all know me, from the least of them unto the greatest of them, saith the LORD: for I will forgive their iniquity, and I will remember their sin no more.

Mat 6:12 And forgive us our debts, as we forgive our debtors.

Mat 6:14 For if ye forgive men their trespasses, your heavenly Father will also forgive you:

Mat 6:15 But if ye forgive not men their trespasses, neither will your Father forgive your trespasses.

Mat 18:32 Then his lord, after that he had called him, said unto him, O thou wicked servant, I forgave thee all that debt, because thou desiredst me:

Mat 18:33 Shouldest not thou also have had compassion on thy fellowservant, even as I had pity on thee?

Mat 18:34 And his lord was wroth, and delivered him to the tormentors, till he should pay all that was due unto him.

Mat 18:35 So likewise shall my heavenly Father do also unto you, if ye from your hearts forgive not every one his brother their trespasses.

Luk 6:37 Judge not, and ye shall not be judged: condemn not, and ye shall not be condemned: forgive, and ye shall be forgiven:

Luk 17:3 Take heed to yourselves: If thy brother trespass against thee, rebuke him; and if he repent, forgive him.

Luk 17:4 And if he trespass against thee seven times in a day, and seven times in a day turn again to thee, saying, I repent; thou shalt forgive him.

Eph 4:32 And be ye kind one to another, tenderhearted, forgiving one another, even as God for Christ's sake hath forgiven you.

Col 1:14 In whom we have redemption through his blood, *even* the forgiveness of sins:

Col 3:13 Forbearing one another, and forgiving one another, if any man have a quarrel against any: even as Christ forgave you, so also *do* ye.

Mercy

SIMPLY PUT MERCY IS pardoning someone who has done wrong the punishment that is due them; or it is giving them a lesser punishment than deserved. The Lord is full of mercy toward his creation. Over and over again in the scriptures we are told to love our neighbor as ourselves, one of the ways we do that is to overlook the wrongs that have been done against us by shewing mercy.

If I was to make a wager, I'd say the bible chapter with the most mentions of the word mercy would be Psalms 136 or Psalms 119 (which is the longest Psalm in the bible and probably the longest chapter as well). Psalms 136 is a Psalm of praise to the Lord and remembering of his works (especially toward Israel and there deliverance from Egypt).

As Christians, it is paramount that we shew mercy to those who have wronged us for our Lord says that if we don't forgive, we wont be forgiven. James seems to later reiterate this when he says "For he shall have judgment without mercy, that hath shewed no mercy; and mercy rejoiceth against judgment."

One distinguishing mark of a Christian (and the Christian faith as a whole for that matter), is that we are merciful (well, we ought to be, anyway). The book of Romans paints a very clear picture that we are not to take revenge for the wrongs done to us but to trust in the Lord, for vengeance belongs to him. It is when we trust in the Lord that he will do what is right, that we can let go and forgive others for their behavior toward us.

Their are probably several and/ or many religions out there that oppose mercy, Evolution/Atheism for one. For under that worldview the horrendous act of abortion is seen as good, or at least permissible. Islam is another, speaking in general terms (there are exceptions), Muslims are instructed by their religion to subjugate the world; convert or die, kill apostates, just to name a few disturbing facts. In the case of Hinduism self-flagellation is a thing during the festival of Charak, this is unmerciful to oneself. Do I even need to mention religions such as satanism, witchcraft, etc.

Exo 33:19 And he said, I will make all my goodness pass before thee, and I will proclaim the name of the LORD before thee; and will be gracious to whom I will be gracious, and will shew mercy on whom I will shew mercy.

Exo 34:7 Keeping mercy for thousands, forgiving iniquity and transgression and sin, and that will by no means clear the guilty; visiting the iniquity of the fathers upon the children, and upon the children's children, unto the third and to the fourth generation.

Num 14:19 Pardon, I beseech thee, the iniquity of this people according unto the greatness of thy mercy, and as thou hast forgiven this people, from Egypt even until now.

Deu 5:10 And shewing mercy unto thousands of them that love me and keep my commandments.

Job 37:13 He causeth it to come, whether for correction, or for his land, or for mercy.

Psa 6:2 Have mercy upon me, O LORD; for I am weak: O LORD, heal me; for my bones are vexed.

Psa 9:13 Have mercy upon me, O LORD; consider my trouble which I suffer of them that hate me, thou that liftest me up from the gates of death:

Psa 13:5 But I have trusted in thy mercy; my heart shall rejoice in thy salvation.

Psa 25:10 All the paths of the LORD are mercy and truth unto such as keep his covenant and his testimonies.

Psa 37:21 The wicked borroweth, and payeth not again: but the righteous sheweth mercy, and giveth.

Psa 145:8 The LORD is gracious, and full of compassion; slow to anger, and of great mercy.

Psa 147:11 The LORD taketh pleasure in them that fear him, in those that hope in his mercy.

Pro 3:3 Let not mercy and truth forsake thee: bind them about thy neck; write them upon the table of thine heart:

Pro_14:21 He that despiseth his neighbour sinneth: but he that hath mercy on the poor, happy is he.

Pro 14:22 Do they not err that devise evil? but mercy and truth shall be to them that devise good.

Jer 31:20 Is Ephraim my dear son? is he a pleasant child? for since I spake against him, I do earnestly remember him still: therefore my bowels are troubled for him; I will surely have mercy upon him, saith the LORD.

Hos 6:6 For I desired mercy, and not sacrifice; and the knowledge of God more than burnt offerings.

Mat 5:7 Blessed are the merciful: for they shall obtain mercy.

Mat 9:13 But go ye and learn what that meaneth, I will have mercy, and not sacrifice: for I am not come to call the righteous, but sinners to repentance.

Mat 9:27 And when Jesus departed thence, two blind men followed him, crying, and saying, Thou Son of David, have mercy on us.

Mat 12:7 But if ye had known what this meaneth, I will have mercy, and not sacrifice, ye would not have condemned the guiltless.

Luk 1:78 Through the tender mercy of our God; whereby the dayspring from on high hath visited us,

Luk 10:37 And he said, He that shewed mercy on him. Then said Jesus unto him, Go, and do thou likewise.

Jas 2:13 For he shall have judgment without mercy, that hath shewed no mercy; and mercy rejoiceth against judgment.

Jas 3:17 But the wisdom that is from above is first pure, then peaceable, gentle, and easy to be intreated, full of mercy and good fruits, without partiality, and without hypocrisy.

1Pe 2:10 Which in time past were not a people, but are now the people of God: which had not obtained mercy, but now have obtained mercy.

Jud 1:2 Mercy unto you, and peace, and love, be multiplied.

Jud 1:21 Keep yourselves in the love of God, looking for the mercy of our Lord Jesus Christ unto eternal life.

Honour Parents

SO WHY IS IMPORTANT for us to honour our parents? Parents are the imagers of God to their children. People can get a warped view of who God is by how their parents treat them. God has placed certain people in our life that although they are our equals in worth, still have authority over us. In our earliest stages of life, our parents are the first people designated by our creator to have rule over us. Later in life we are to subject ourselves to other authorities in their proper order (employers, governors, presidents, etc); however the rule of God in our lives must trump them all. Although parents should treat their kids after a godly manner, it is the children's responsibility to submit to their parents instructions.

The bible says that we are to train up a child in the way he should go, and when he is older he will not depart from it. As people get older they tend to get set in their ways and it becomes much harder in most instances to change their ways, this is why it's important to raise your offspring to be of godly character. It could save them a lot of sorrow later on. Some experiences are best not to learn firsthand such as drugs, promiscuity, laziness, etc.

We see in Scripture in both old and new testaments that we are to honor our parents (Exodus 20:12), however honor doesn't always equal obey. Children are to obey their parents (Ephesians 6:1), but there comes a time when we strike out on our own and start our own families in which, at that time we are still to honor our parents but not necessarily obey them. I'm speaking in such cases as if/when our parents entice us to sin. When that happens we are to follow God and not men.

What are some instances when parents might entice their children to sin. Well, how about I give just five examples of such cases that I believe are quite common in the U.S. Now before I list these five reasons I just want to state that I don't expect the reader to agree with me on all five of these points as all of us Christians are at different levels in our sanctification. Furthermore, I don't claim to be omniscient, I am fallible just like everyone else, However after a considerable amount study on these five subjects I personally am convinced that these are areas where many Christians sin frequently and they are:

1. **Observing of Pagan Holidays**
2. **The Taking of Pharmakeia (drugs)**
3. **Mothers enticing their daughters into the workforce.**
4. **Enticing young adults to go into debt.**
5. **Parents who teach kids to prioritize things (money, sports, etc) over God, aka Idolatry.**

NOW AM I SAYING NOT to care for our parents? Certainly not, for scripture instructs us to requite our parents (1 Timothy 5:4), and even admonishes against not doing ought for our parents (Mark 7:10-13). Cursing your parents was a death sentence back in the Old Testament (Exodus 21:17). So in summary love and honour your parents; obey them when your young but if they tell you to sin, that is where you draw the line. It is ok to set boundaries.

Exo 20:12 Honour thy father and thy mother: that thy days may be long upon the land which the LORD thy God giveth thee.

Exo 21:17 And he that curseth his father, or his mother, shall surely be put to death.

Lev 19:3 Ye shall fear every man his mother, and his father, and keep my sabbaths: I *am* the LORD your God.

Deu 5:16 Honour thy father and thy mother, as the LORD thy God hath commanded thee; that thy days may be prolonged, and that it may go well with thee, in the land which the LORD thy God giveth thee.

Deu 27:16 Cursed *be* he that setteth light by his father or his mother. And all the people shall say, Amen.

Pro 30:17 The eye *that* mocketh at *his* father, and despiseth to obey *his* mother, the ravens of the valley shall pick it out, and the young eagles shall eat it.

Eze 22:7 In thee have they set light by father and mother: in the midst of thee have they dealt by oppression with the stranger: in thee have they vexed the fatherless and the widow.

Mat 15:4 For God commanded, saying, Honour thy father and mother: and, He that curseth father or mother, let him die the death.

Mar 7:9 And he said unto them, Full well ye reject the commandment of God, that ye may keep your own tradition.

Mar 7:10 For Moses said, Honour thy father and thy mother; and, Whoso curseth father or mother, let him die the death:

Mar 7:11 But ye say, If a man shall say to his father or mother, *It is* Corban, that is to say, a gift, by whatsoever thou mightest be profited by me; *he shall be free.*

Mar 7:12 And ye suffer him no more to do ought for his father or his mother;

Mar 7:13 Making the word of God of none effect through your tradition, which ye have delivered: and many such like things do ye.

Rom 1:30 Backbiters, haters of God, despiteful, proud, boasters, inventors of evil things, disobedient to parents,

Eph 6:1 Children, obey your parents in the Lord: for this is right.

Eph 6:2 Honour thy father and mother; (which is the first commandment with promise;)

Eph 6:3 That it may be well with thee, and thou mayest live long on the earth.

1Ti 5:4 But if any widow have children or nephews, let them learn first to shew piety at home, and to requite their parents: for that is good and acceptable before God.

Peace

A QUOTE FROM WEBSTERS Revised Unabridged Dictionary 1913 "Peace ...A state of quiet or tranquility; freedom from disturbance or agitation; calm; repose; specifically: (a) Exemption from, or cessation of, war with public enemies. (b) Public quiet, order, and contentment in obedience to law. (c) Exemption from, or subjection of, agitating passions; tranquility of mind or conscience. (d) Reconciliation; agreement after variance; harmony; concord..."

If you are feeling tired and restless, worn down with the troubles of life, full of care, worry, anxiety, and fear; may I make a suggestion. Go to Jesus, he is the prince of peace and we are to cast all our care on him, for he cares for us. Only Jesus can give us true peace. The bible is clear that those that love God's law have great peace, peace is added to them that remember the law and keeping the commandments adds peace.

The bible says that we are to live peaceably with all men (as much as lieth in us) and to be peace makers not peace keepers. Peace keepers avoid conflict by holding in their convictions, feelings, and disagreements so as to not rock the boat. It is passive. Whereas peacemakers proactively try to resolve both outer and inner turmoil with the opposing party. They try to come to a resolution and not avoid the conflict. They speak truth in love. Peace is a fruit of the Spirit.

We read twice in the book of Isaiah that there is no peace to the wicked, and the same prophet likens the wicked to a troubled sea, when it cannot rest. You see mankind has been given what we call a conscience; The Latin word (con) means with and the Latin word (scientia) means knowledge. We know right from wrong because God has placed it in our hearts (Romans 2:14-15).

In my opinion, this is probably why many different religions have at least some common views of morality. For instance adultery is frowned upon in many different faiths including but not limited to Judaism, Christianity, Catholicism, 7th day Adventism, and Jehovah's witnesses; while this can be attributed to the fact that all the aforementioned religions share most of the same scriptures the following faiths are vastly different from these first ones and have different religious text. Islam (in certain instances), Buddhism, and Jainism just to name a few. All these major world religions shun adultery.

Listening to your conscience is vital if you want to have peace, this is because although the bible is a great moral rule book it doesn't list every possible bad thing you can do. For instance Necrophilia, Heroine use, and pranking your family may not be specifically stated by name as a sin in scripture (though you may use indirect verses to prove their unlawfulness), but this doesn't mean you should do them. The bible is clear that we ought not to sin against our conscience. Remember God has not given you a spirit of fear but of love, power and a sound mind.

Deu 20:10 When thou comest nigh unto a city to fight against it, then proclaim peace unto it.

Deu 20:11 And it shall be, if it make thee answer of peace, and open unto thee, then it shall be, *that* all the people *that is* found therein shall be tributaries unto thee, and they shall serve thee.

Deu 20:12 And if it will make no peace with thee, but will make war against thee, then thou shalt besiege it:

Deu 29:19 And it come to pass, when he heareth the words of this curse, that he bless himself in his heart, saying, I shall have peace, though I walk in the imagination of mine heart, to add drunkenness to thirst:

2Ki 9:22 And it came to pass, when Joram saw Jehu, that he said, *Is it* peace, Jehu? And he answered, What peace, so long as the whoredoms of thy mother Jezebel and her witchcrafts *are so* many?

2Ch 18:26 And say, Thus saith the king, Put this *fellow* in the prison, and feed him with bread of affliction and with water of affliction, until I return in peace.

2Ch 18:27 And Micaiah said, If thou certainly return in peace, *then* hath not the LORD spoken by me. And he said, Hearken, all ye people.

Psa 34:14 Depart from evil, and do good; seek peace, and pursue it.

Psa 119:165 Great peace have they which love thy law: and nothing shall offend them.

Pro 3:2 For length of days, and long life, and peace, shall they add to thee.

Pro 16:7 When a man's ways please the LORD, he maketh even his enemies to be at peace with him.

Ecc 3:8 A time to love, and a time to hate; a time of war, and a time of peace.

Isa 9:6 For unto us a child is born, unto us a son is given: and the government shall be upon his shoulder: and his name shall be called Wonderful, Counsellor, The mighty God, The everlasting Father, The Prince of Peace.

Isa_26:3 Thou wilt keep *him* in perfect peace, *whose* mind *is* stayed *on thee:* because he trusteth in thee.

Isa 48:22 *There is* no peace, saith the LORD, unto the wicked.

Isa 54:13 And all thy children *shall be* taught of the LORD; and great *shall be* the peace of thy children.

Isa 55:12 For ye shall go out with joy, and be led forth with peace: the mountains and the hills shall break forth before you into singing, and all the trees of the field shall clap *their* hands.

Isa 59:8 The way of peace they know not; and *there is* no judgment in their goings: they have made them crooked paths: whosoever goeth therein shall not know peace.

Jer 16:5 For thus saith the LORD, Enter not into the house of mourning, neither go to lament nor bemoan them: for I have taken away my peace from this people, saith the LORD, *even* lovingkindness and mercies.

Jer 28:9 The prophet which prophesieth of peace, when the word of the prophet shall come to pass, *then* shall the prophet be known, that the LORD hath truly sent him.

Jer 29:11 For I know the thoughts that I think toward you, saith the LORD, thoughts of peace, and not of evil, to give you an expected end.

Mat 5:9 Blessed *are* the peacemakers: for they shall be called the children of God.

Mat 10:13 And if the house be worthy, let your peace come upon it: but if it be not worthy, let your peace return to you.

Mat 10:34 Think not that I am come to send peace on earth: I came not to send peace, but a sword.

Joh 14:27 Peace I leave with you, my peace I give unto you: not as the world giveth, give I unto you. Let not your heart be troubled, neither let it be afraid.

Joh 16:33 These things I have spoken unto you, that in me ye might have peace. In the world ye shall have tribulation: but be of good cheer; I have overcome the world.

Rom 5:1 Therefore being justified by faith, we have peace with God through our Lord Jesus Christ:

Rom 10:15 And how shall they preach, except they be sent? as it is written, How beautiful are the feet of them that preach the gospel of peace, and bring glad tidings of good things!

Rom 12:18 If it be possible, as much as lieth in you, live peaceably with all men.

Rom 14:17 For the kingdom of God is not meat and drink; but righteousness, and peace, and joy in the Holy Ghost.

2Co 13:11 Finally, brethren, farewell. Be perfect, be of good comfort, be of one mind, live in peace; and the God of love and peace shall be with you.

Gal 5:22 But the fruit of the Spirit is love, joy, peace, longsuffering, gentleness, goodness, faith,

Eph 2:14 For he is our peace, who hath made both one, and hath broken down the middle wall of partition *between us;*

Eph 2:15 Having abolished in his flesh the enmity, *even* the law of commandments *contained* in ordinances; for to make in himself of twain one new man, *so* making peace;

Heb 12:14 Follow peace with all *men,* and holiness, without which no man shall see the Lord:

Jas 3:18 And the fruit of righteousness is sown in peace of them that make peace.

Trust

WHAT IS TRUST? TRUST is placing confidence and reliance upon someone. When we trust in the Lord it can be seen as us believing that he will do what is in our best interest. That he will come through in even the most dire circumstances, even if it isn't in a way we expect; and it just so happens things don't go the way we wanted, we will acknowledge the Lord's omniscience; in that he knows what he is doing, and it was for the best.

The bible tells us not to trust in ourselves, not in our heart, not in horses, not in men, and not in riches. We are to place our confidence in the Lord and his ways. The Lord is our healer, we are not to trust in doctors. Is it a sin to visit a physician? In some instances no. It is this authors conviction that to get tested for disease such as diabetes, or some other ailment is not sinful. It wouldn't be sinful in my opinion to get a bullet removed, a bone set, or stitches. However, we are not to trust in doctors prognostications, nor should we take pharmaceuticals (witchcraft). Instead we should rely primarily on the Lord first and foremost and guidance from him on how we should go about seeking to get better.

Another major way people do not trust the Lord is in provision. We are not to trust in our employer or the government as our providers, now is it a sin to have a job, or to ask for assistance; I would say no, it isn't a sin. But ultimately our resources come from God and when things look bleak aka a job loss, we shouldn't fret over our financial situation; again trusting in riches is bad (in fact it can bar you from everlasting life). There are many more verses in the scriptures I could've cited for the bible topic of trust, but for the sake of space I am only going to list a small number of them.

Jdg 9:15 And the bramble said unto the trees, If in truth ye anoint me king over you, *then* come *and* put your trust in my shadow: and if not, let fire come out of the bramble, and devour the cedars of Lebanon.

2Sa 22:3 The God of my rock; in him will I trust: *he is* my shield, and the horn of my salvation, my high tower, and my refuge, my saviour; thou savest me from violence.

Job 13:15 Though he slay me, yet will I trust in him: but I will maintain mine own ways before him.

Psa 2:12 Kiss the Son, lest he be angry, and ye perish *from* the way, when his wrath is kindled but a little. Blessed *are* all they that put their trust in him.

Psa 37:3 Trust in the LORD, and do good; *so* shalt thou dwell in the land, and verily thou shalt be fed.

Psa 40:4 Blessed *is* that man that maketh the LORD his trust, and respecteth not the proud, nor such as turn aside to lies.

Psa 56:11 In God have I put my trust: I will not be afraid what man can do unto me.

Psa 118:8 *It is* better to trust in the LORD than to put confidence in man.

Psa 118:9 *It is* better to trust in the LORD than to put confidence in princes.

Pro 3:5 Trust in the LORD with all thine heart; and lean not unto thine own understanding.

Pro 28:26 He that trusteth in his own heart is a fool: but whoso walketh wisely, he shall be delivered.

Pro 29:25 The fear of man bringeth a snare: but whoso putteth his trust in the LORD shall be safe.

Jer 17:5 Thus saith the LORD; Cursed *be* the man that trusteth in man, and maketh flesh his arm, and whose heart departeth from the LORD.

Jer 17:7 Blessed *is* the man that trusteth in the LORD, and whose hope the LORD is.

Hos 10:13 Ye have plowed wickedness, ye have reaped iniquity; ye have eaten the fruit of lies: because thou didst trust in thy way, in the multitude of thy mighty men.

Mic 7:5 Trust ye not in a friend, put ye not confidence in a guide: keep the doors of thy mouth from her that lieth in thy bosom.

Nah 1:7 The LORD *is* good, a strong hold in the day of trouble; and he knoweth them that trust in him.

Hab 2:18 What profiteth the graven image that the maker thereof hath graven it; the molten image, and a teacher of lies, that the maker of his work trusteth therein, to make dumb idols?

Chapter 3: More Benevolent and / or Important Topics

Baptism

What is baptism? Well in the gospels we see John the baptist was baptizing with water unto repentance. John was doing this so that the Messiah would be made manifest to Israel. It is a biblical command to water baptize people (Mat 28), however water baptism does not save anyone. How does one reach that conclusion? The thief on the cross wasn't water baptized (to the best of our knowledge), people in the book of acts received the Spirit before water baptism, and Simon the sorcerer was water baptized in Acts 8 but he doesn't appear to be regenerate. We see in 1st Corinthians that Paul wasn't sent to baptize, why not if it saves? Those are a few reasons I believe water baptism, although important, doesn't save anyone. It is the Spirit baptism that puts one into the body of Christ (Rom 8:9, 1 Cor 12:13).

What does Baptism represent. Being submerged in water represents you being buried with Christ, then coming out of the water is the representation of being born again, or made new. It is a public declaration that you are a Christian and that you have been changed. Just because water baptism isn't necessary for salvation doesn't mean it should be avoided. I don't want anyone to feel discouraged from doing it, for it is a biblical command, and if one is a true believer then they will want to obey the scripture.

Other things the bible says about baptism include:...

· **There is one baptism**

· **Jesus had to endure another baptism, which at least two of his disciples did as well. Some refer to it as the baptism of suffering**

· **Belief in Jesus is a prerequisite to baptism, (infant baptism is a no no).**

· **Baptism is done in the name of Jesus.**

Mat 3:11 I indeed baptize you with water unto repentance: but he that cometh after me is mightier than I, whose shoes I am not worthy to bear: he shall baptize you with the Holy Ghost, and *with* fire:

Mat 20:22 But Jesus answered and said, Ye know not what ye ask. Are ye able to drink of the cup that I shall drink of, and to be baptized with the baptism that I am baptized with? They say unto him, We are able.

Mat 20:23 And he saith unto them, Ye shall drink indeed of my cup, and be baptized with the baptism that I am baptized with: but to sit on my right hand, and on my left, is not mine to give, but *it shall be given to them* for whom it is prepared of my Father.

Mat 21:25 The baptism of John, whence was it? from heaven, or of men? And they reasoned with themselves, saying, If we shall say, From heaven;

Mat 28:19 Go ye therefore, and teach all nations, baptizing them in the name of the Father, and of the Son, and of the Holy Ghost:

Mar 1:9 And it came to pass in those days, that Jesus came from Nazareth of Galilee, and was baptized of John in Jordan.

Mar 16:16 He that believeth and is baptized shall be saved; but he that believeth not shall be damned.

Luk 3:3 And he came into all the country about Jordan, preaching the baptism of repentance for the remission of sins;

Luk 12:50 But I have a baptism to be baptized with; and how am I straitened till it be accomplished!

Joh 1:31 And I knew him not: but that he should be made manifest to Israel, therefore am I come baptizing with water.

Joh 1:33 And I knew him not: but he that sent me to baptize with water, the same said unto me, Upon whom thou shalt see the Spirit descending, and remaining on him, the same is he which baptizeth with the Holy Ghost.

Joh 3:23 And John also was baptizing in Aenon near to Salim, because there was much water there: and they came, and were baptized.

Joh 4:1 When therefore the Lord knew how the Pharisees had heard that Jesus made and baptized more disciples than John,

Joh 4:2 (Though Jesus himself baptized not, but his disciples,)

Act 1:5 For John truly baptized with water; but ye shall be baptized with the Holy Ghost not many days hence.

Act 2:38 Then Peter said unto them, Repent, and be baptized every one of you in the name of Jesus Christ for the remission of sins, and ye shall receive the gift of the Holy Ghost.

Act 8:16 (For as yet he was fallen upon none of them: only they were baptized in the name of the Lord Jesus.)

Act 8:36 And as they went on *their* way, they came unto a certain water: and the eunuch said, See, *here is* water; what doth hinder me to be baptized?

Act 8:37 And Philip said, If thou believest with all thine heart, thou mayest. And he answered and said, I believe that Jesus Christ is the Son of God.

Act 10:47 Can any man forbid water, that these should not be baptized, which have received the Holy Ghost as well as we?

Act 10:48 And he commanded them to be baptized in the name of the Lord. Then prayed they him to tarry certain days.

Act 18:24 And a certain Jew named Apollos, born at Alexandria, an eloquent man, *and* mighty in the scriptures, came to Ephesus.

Act 18:25 This man was instructed in the way of the Lord; and being fervent in the spirit, he spake and taught diligently the things of the Lord, knowing only the baptism of John.

Act 18:26 And he began to speak boldly in the synagogue: whom when Aquila and Priscilla had heard, they took him unto *them,* and expounded unto him the way of God more perfectly.

Act 19:3 And he said unto them, Unto what then were ye baptized? And they said, Unto John's baptism.

Act 19:4 Then said Paul, John verily baptized with the baptism of repentance, saying unto the people, that they should believe on him which should come after him, that is, on Christ Jesus.

Act 19:5 When they heard *this,* they were baptized in the name of the Lord Jesus.

Act 22:16 And now why tarriest thou? arise, and be baptized, and wash away thy sins, calling on the name of the Lord.

Rom 6:3 Know ye not, that so many of us as were baptized into Jesus Christ were baptized into his death?

Rom 6:4 Therefore we are buried with him by baptism into death: that like as Christ was raised up from the dead by the glory of the Father, even so we also should walk in newness of life.

1Co 1:13 Is Christ divided? was Paul crucified for you? or were ye baptized in the name of Paul?

1Co 1:14 I thank God that I baptized none of you, but Crispus and Gaius;

1Co 1:15 Lest any should say that I had baptized in mine own name.

1Co 1:16 And I baptized also the household of Stephanas: besides, I know not whether I baptized any other.

1Co 1:17 For Christ sent me not to baptize, but to preach the gospel: not with wisdom of words, lest the cross of Christ should be made of none effect.

1Co 12:13 For by one Spirit are we all baptized into one body, whether *we be* Jews or Gentiles, whether *we be* bond or free; and have been all made to drink into one Spirit.

1Co 15:29 Else what shall they do which are baptized for the dead, if the dead rise not at all? why are they then baptized for the dead?

Gal 3:27 For as many of you as have been baptized into Christ have put on Christ.

Eph 4:5 One Lord, one faith, one baptism,

Col 2:12 Buried with him in baptism, wherein also ye are risen with *him* through the faith of the operation of God, who hath raised him from the dead.

1Pe 3:21 The like figure whereunto *even* baptism doth also now save us (not the putting away of the filth of the flesh, but the answer of a good conscience toward God,) by the resurrection of Jesus Christ:

Five passages that refute Baptismal Regeneration

Below are five reasons why water baptism saves not. I already mentioned the reasons in Luke 23 and Acts 8 before so I need not restate it here. In addition to those two reasons I list three more below. In Luke seven we see that the women who washed Jesus feet was saved by her faith and she wasn't baptized; though this isn't the best evidence because it doesn't say she wasn't either. In Luke 13 we see that Abraham, Isaac, and Jacob was not baptized yet they were saved, and of course in Ephesians 2 we know that we are not saved by our works.

Luk 7:50 And he said to the woman, Thy faith hath saved thee; go in peace.

Luk 13:28 There shall be weeping and gnashing of teeth, when ye shall see Abraham, and Isaac, and Jacob, and all the prophets, in the kingdom of God, and you yourselves thrust out.

Luk 23:43 And Jesus said unto him, Verily I say unto thee, To day shalt thou be with me in paradise.

Act 8:21 Thou hast neither part nor lot in this matter: for thy heart is not right in the sight of God.

Act 8:22 Repent therefore of this thy wickedness, and pray God, if perhaps the thought of thine heart may be forgiven thee.

Eph 2:8 For by grace are ye saved through faith; and that not of yourselves: *it is* the gift of God:

Eph 2:9 Not of works, lest any man should boast.

Old Testament Miracles

HERE IS A COMPILATION of numerous miracles recorded throughout the Old Testament. Some of these are plagues that the Lord brought upon the Egyptians, others are describing how God sustained and/or punished the Israelites in the wilderness, there are also the miraculous events surrounding the life of Joshua and Elijah recorded here as well, just fyi this may not be a complete list.

Allow me to take a moment to go into detail about some of the different types of miracles we see in the bible, some of the miracles we see in scripture which caused or were used to cause destruction such as: the ten plagues of Egypt (as I just stated); this consist of flies, lice, boils, blood water, darkness, a murrain (death of cattle/livestock), frogs, locusts, hail, and the death of the firstborn. This is not in order. Fire falling from heaven and destroying people, the sun stood still, and the falling of Jericho walls, to name a few.

There where some miracles used to sustain life such as delivering the Israelites by the splitting of the red sea, and giving them water from a rock. Manna that rained down six days a week, a resurrected child, and bitter water made sweet.

There where a couple of miracles at least that were done to settle a debt such as the swimming (floating) axe, and multiplication of oil in vessels. These are but a sample of the Miracles we see throughout the Old Testament...oh and let's not forget about Balaam's ass.

Exo 7:20 And Moses and Aaron did so, as the LORD commanded; and he lifted up the rod, and smote the waters that *were* in the river, in the sight of Pharaoh, and in the sight of his servants; and all the waters that *were* in the river were turned to blood.

Exo 8:6 And Aaron stretched out his hand over the waters of Egypt; and the frogs came up, and covered the land of Egypt.

Exo 8:17 And they did so; for Aaron stretched out his hand with his rod, and smote the dust of the earth, and it became lice in man, and in beast; all the dust of the land became lice throughout all the land of Egypt.

Exo 9:6 And the LORD did that thing on the morrow, and all the cattle of Egypt died: but of the cattle of the children of Israel died not one.

Exo 9:10 And they took ashes of the furnace, and stood before Pharaoh; and Moses sprinkled it up toward heaven; and it became a boil breaking forth *with* blains upon man, and upon beast.

Exo 9:23 And Moses stretched forth his rod toward heaven: and the LORD sent thunder and hail, and the fire ran along upon the ground; and the LORD rained hail upon the land of Egypt.

Exo 10:13 And Moses stretched forth his rod over the land of Egypt, and the LORD brought an east wind upon the land all that day, and all *that* night; *and* when it was morning, the east wind brought the locusts.

Exo 10:21 And the LORD said unto Moses, Stretch out thine hand toward heaven, that there may be darkness over the land of Egypt, even darkness *which* may be felt.

Exo 12:29 And it came to pass, that at midnight the LORD smote all the firstborn in the land of Egypt, from the firstborn of Pharaoh that sat on his throne unto the firstborn of the captive that *was* in the dungeon; and all the firstborn of cattle.

Exo 13:21 And the LORD went before them by day in a pillar of a cloud, to lead them the way; and by night in a pillar of fire, to give them light; to go by day and night:

Exo 15:25 And he cried unto the LORD; and the LORD shewed him a tree, *which* when he had cast into the waters, the waters were made sweet: there he made for them a statute and an ordinance, and there he proved them,

Exo 16:4 Then said the LORD unto Moses, Behold, I will rain bread from heaven for you; and the people shall go out and gather a certain rate every day, that I may prove them, whether they will walk in my law, or no.

Exo 17:6 Behold, I will stand before thee there upon the rock in Horeb; and thou shalt smite the rock, and there shall come water out of it, that the people may drink. And Moses did so in the sight of the elders of Israel.

Exo 19:18 And mount Sinai was altogether on a smoke, because the LORD descended upon it in fire: and the smoke thereof ascended as the smoke of a furnace, and the whole mount quaked greatly.

Num 16:32 And the earth opened her mouth, and swallowed them up, and their houses, and all the men that *appertained* unto Korah, and all *their* goods.

Num 21:9 And Moses made a serpent of brass, and put it upon a pole, and it came to pass, that if a serpent had bitten any man, when he beheld the serpent of brass, he lived.

Jos 3:16 That the waters which came down from above stood *and* rose up upon an heap very far from the city Adam, that *is* beside Zaretan: and those that came down toward the sea of the plain, *even* the salt sea, failed, *and* were cut off: and the people passed over right against Jericho.

Jos 6:20 So the people shouted when *the priests* blew with the trumpets: and it came to pass, when the people heard the sound of the trumpet, and the people shouted with a great shout, that the wall fell down flat, so that the people went up into the city, every man straight before him, and they took the city.

Jos 10:13 And the sun stood still, and the moon stayed, until the people had avenged themselves upon their enemies. *Is* not this written in the book of Jasher? So the sun stood still in the midst of heaven, and hasted not to go down about a whole day.

Jdg 16:30 And Samson said, Let me die with the Philistines. And he bowed himself with *all his* might; and the house fell upon the lords, and upon all the people that *were* therein. So the dead which he slew at his death were more than *they* which he slew in his life.

2Ki 1:10 And Elijah answered and said to the captain of fifty, If I *be* a man of God, then let fire come down from heaven, and consume thee and thy fifty. And there came down fire from heaven, and consumed him and his fifty.

2Ki 2:8 And Elijah took his mantle, and wrapped *it* together, and smote the waters, and they were divided hither and thither, so that they two went over on dry ground.

2Ki 2:11 And it came to pass, as they still went on, and talked, that, behold, *there appeared* a chariot of fire, and horses of fire, and parted them both asunder; and Elijah went up by a whirlwind into heaven.

2Ki 4:4 And when thou art come in, thou shalt shut the door upon thee and upon thy sons, and shalt pour out into all those vessels, and thou shalt set aside that which is full.

2Ki 4:43 And his servitor said, What, should I set this before an hundred men? He said again, Give the people, that they may eat: for thus saith the LORD, They shall eat, and shall leave *thereof.*

2Ki 5:14 Then went he down, and dipped himself seven times in Jordan, according to the saying of the man of God: and his flesh came again like unto the flesh of a little child, and he was clean.

2Ki 6:6 And the man of God said, Where fell it? And he shewed him the place. And he cut down a stick, and cast *it* in thither; and the iron did swim.

2Ki 6:17 And Elisha prayed, and said, LORD, I pray thee, open his eyes, that he may see. And the LORD opened the eyes of the young man; and he saw: and, behold, the mountain *was* full of horses and chariots of fire round about Elisha.

Psa 78:43 How he had wrought his signs in Egypt, and his wonders in the field of Zoan:

Psa 78:44 And had turned their rivers into blood; and their floods, that they could not drink.

Isa 7:14 Therefore the Lord himself shall give you a sign; Behold, a virgin shall conceive, and bear a son, and shall call his name Immanuel.

Eze 1:4 And I looked, and, behold, a whirlwind came out of the north, a great cloud, and a fire infolding itself, and a brightness *was* about it, and out of the midst thereof as the colour of amber, out of the midst of the fire.

Eze 1:5 Also out of the midst thereof *came* the likeness of four living creatures. And this *was* their appearance; they had the likeness of a man.

Eze 1:6 And every one had four faces, and every one had four wings.

Dan 2:30 But as for me, this secret is not revealed to me for *any* wisdom that I have more than any living, but for *their* sakes that shall make known the interpretation to the king, and that thou mightest know the thoughts of thy heart.

Dan 3:27 And the princes, governors, and captains, and the king's counsellors, being gathered together, saw these men, upon whose bodies the fire had no power, nor was an hair of their head singed, neither were their coats changed, nor the smell of fire had passed on them.

Joe 2:28 And it shall come to pass afterward, *that* I will pour out my spirit upon all flesh; and your sons and your daughters shall prophesy, your old men shall dream dreams, your young men shall see visions:

Zec 14:12 And this shall be the plague wherewith the LORD will smite all the people that have fought against Jerusalem; Their flesh shall consume away while they stand upon their feet, and their eyes shall consume away in their holes, and their tongue shall consume away in their mouth.

New Testament Miracles

THE FOLLOWING ARE NEARLY 50 New Testament recordings of Miracles by Jesus and his disciples. Primarily they are miracles of healing, but also there are deliverances from unclean spirits. There are also some other miraculous events recorded such as Jesus walking on water, multiplication of food, and raising from the dead as well. (please note that this list will not cover everything Jesus did (see John 21:25).

Before we get to this list, why don't I take a moment to go over some of the miraculous events of my life or rather those that are closest to me. There are many skeptics out there who doubt that God exists, whether atheist or agnostic it can be a little disheartening to see them reject the truth when you present them with the gospel and even evidence of God's hand in your life. With that said here are a few examples of personal testimonies put very briefly from my family.

My wife once had swine flu and a fever, and after hearing a minister praying for those with said ailment and praying in agreement with him was healed almost instantly. There was another instance when my wife was a teen (before we were married) that she had epilepsy(a disease I might add has no known cure), well all that changed when they had some elders of the church come over and pray over her. She hasn't had a seizure in about 20 years.

There was another time when some of my wife's relatives had a bunch of guest over for dinner but only had enough food prepared for 4 or 5 people. Well the server just didn't look into the pot but instead exercised faith and gave everyone a hearty portion, They served approximately 12-16 people.

When it came time to refill his propane tank, the guy who showed up to do it said it was already full. But my dad had been using the propane for a long time, where did all that extra propane come from? I had a sister-in-the-Lord who sometimes has the ability to see things spiritually.

That is all the examples that I am going list here of miracles, sure I have testimonies of relatives seeing apparitions but I believe most of those cases were probably demonic in nature; so they would be out of place for this topic. If anyone wants to see more evidence of the supernatural, I would recommend YouTube, there are no shortage of churches and ministers operating in the gifts of the Spirit. Whether the word of knowledge, or of wisdom, or whether tongues, or healing, etc. It shouldn't be hard to find.

Without further delay, here is a list of NT miracles...

1. Mat 8:16 When the even was come, they brought unto him many that were possessed with devils: and he cast out the spirits with *his* word, and healed all that were sick:

2. Mat 9:6 But that ye may know that the Son of man hath power on earth to forgive sins, (then saith he to the sick of the palsy,) Arise, take up thy bed, and go unto thine house.

3. Mat 9:25 But when the people were put forth, he went in, and took her by the hand, and the maid arose.

4. Mat 9:30 And their eyes were opened; and Jesus straitly charged them, saying, See *that* no man know *it*.

5. Mat 9:33 And when the devil was cast out, the dumb spake: and the multitudes marvelled, saying, It was never so seen in Israel.

6. Mat 12:22 Then was brought unto him one possessed with a devil, blind, and dumb: and he healed him, insomuch that the blind and dumb both spake and saw.

7. Mat 15:28 Then Jesus answered and said unto her, O woman, great *is* thy faith: be it unto thee even as thou wilt. And her daughter was made whole from that very hour.

8. Mat 15:38 And they that did eat were four thousand men, beside women and children.

9. Mat 17:27 Notwithstanding, lest we should offend them, go thou to the sea, and cast an hook, and take up the fish that first cometh up; and when thou hast

opened his mouth, thou shalt find a piece of money: that take, and give unto them for me and thee.

10. Mat 20:34 So Jesus had compassion *on them,* and touched their eyes: and immediately their eyes received sight, and they followed him.

11. Mat 21:19 And when he saw a fig tree in the way, he came to it, and found nothing thereon, but leaves only, and said unto it, Let no fruit grow on thee henceforward for ever. And presently the fig tree withered away.

12. Mar 1:25 And Jesus rebuked him, saying, Hold thy peace, and come out of him.

13. Mar 1:31 And he came and took her by the hand, and lifted her up; and immediately the fever left her, and she ministered unto them.

14. Mar 1:42 And as soon as he had spoken, immediately the leprosy departed from him, and he was cleansed.

15. Mar 3:5 And when he had looked round about on them with anger, being grieved for the hardness of their hearts, he saith unto the man, Stretch forth thine hand. And he stretched *it* out: and his hand was restored whole as the other.

16. Mar 5:13 And forthwith Jesus gave them leave. And the unclean spirits went out, and entered into the swine: and the herd ran violently down a steep place into the sea, (they were about two thousand;) and were choked in the sea.

17. Mar 5:29 And straightway the fountain of her blood was dried up; and she felt in *her* body that she was healed of that plague.

18. Mar 6:48 And he saw them toiling in rowing; for the wind was contrary unto them: and about the fourth watch of the night he cometh unto them, walking upon the sea, and would have passed by them.

19. Mar 6:56 And whithersoever he entered, into villages, or cities, or country, they laid the sick in the streets, and besought him that they might touch if it

were but the border of his garment: and as many as touched him were made whole.

20. Mar 7:35 And straightway his ears were opened, and the string of his tongue was loosed, and he spake plain.

21. Mar 8:25 After that he put *his* hands again upon his eyes, and made him look up: and he was restored, and saw every man clearly.

22. Mar 9:25 When Jesus saw that the people came running together, he rebuked the foul spirit, saying unto him, *Thou* dumb and deaf spirit, I charge thee, come out of him, and enter no more into him.

23. Luk 5:7 And they beckoned unto *their* partners, which were in the other ship, that they should come and help them. And they came, and filled both the ships, so that they began to sink.

24. Luk 7:15 And he that was dead sat up, and began to speak. And he delivered him to his mother.

25. Luk 8:24 And they came to him, and awoke him, saying, Master, master, we perish. Then he arose, and rebuked the wind and the raging of the water: and they ceased, and there was a calm.

26. Luk 13:13 And he laid *his* hands on her: and immediately she was made straight, and glorified God.

27. Luk 14:4 And they held their peace. And he took *him,* and healed him, and let him go;

28. Luk 17:14 And when he saw *them,* he said unto them, Go shew yourselves unto the priests. And it came to pass, that, as they went, they were cleansed.

29. Luk 22:51 And Jesus answered and said, Suffer ye thus far. And he touched his ear, and healed him.

30. Joh 2:9 When the ruler of the feast had tasted the water that was made wine, and knew not whence it was: (but the servants which drew the water knew;) the governor of the feast called the bridegroom,

31.Joh 4:47 When he heard that Jesus was come out of Judaea into Galilee, he went unto him, and besought him that he would come down, and heal his son: for he was at the point of death.

32.Joh 5:11 He answered them, He that made me whole, the same said unto me, Take up thy bed, and walk.

33. Joh 6:11 And Jesus took the loaves; and when he had given thanks, he distributed to the disciples, and the disciples to them that were set down; and likewise of the fishes as much as they would.

34. Joh 9:7 And said unto him, Go, wash in the pool of Siloam, (which is by interpretation, Sent.) He went his way therefore, and washed, and came seeing.

35. Joh 11:44 And he that was dead came forth, bound hand and foot with graveclothes: and his face was bound about with a napkin. Jesus saith unto them, Loose him, and let him go.

36.Act 2:4 And they were all filled with the Holy Ghost, and began to speak with other tongues, as the Spirit gave them utterance.

37.Act 2:43 And fear came upon every soul: and many wonders and signs were done by the apostles.

38.Act 3:7 And he took him by the right hand, and lifted *him* up: and immediately his feet and ankle bones received strength.

39.Act 5:12 And by the hands of the apostles were many signs and wonders wrought among the people; (and they were all with one accord in Solomon's porch.

40.Act 5:15 Insomuch that they brought forth the sick into the streets, and laid *them* on beds and couches, that at the least the shadow of Peter passing by might overshadow some of them.

41.Act 5:19 But the angel of the Lord by night opened the prison doors, and brought them forth, and said,

42. Act 9:18 And immediately there fell from his eyes as it had been scales: and he received sight forthwith, and arose, and was baptized.

43. Act 9:34 And Peter said unto him, Aeneas, Jesus Christ maketh thee whole: arise, and make thy bed. And he arose immediately.

44. Act 9:40 But Peter put them all forth, and kneeled down, and prayed; and turning *him* to the body said, Tabitha, arise. And she opened her eyes: and when she saw Peter, she sat up.

45. Act 16:18 And this did she many days. But Paul, being grieved, turned and said to the spirit, I command thee in the name of Jesus Christ to come out of her. And he came out the same hour.

46. Act 20:10 And Paul went down, and fell on him, and embracing *him* said, Trouble not yourselves; for his life is in him.

47. Act 28:5 And he shook off the beast into the fire, and felt no harm.

48. Act 28:8 And it came to pass, that the father of Publius lay sick of a fever and of a bloody flux: to whom Paul entered in, and prayed, and laid his hands on him, and healed him.

49. 1Pe 1:3 Blessed *be* the God and Father of our Lord Jesus Christ, which according to his abundant mercy hath begotten us again unto a lively hope by the resurrection of Jesus Christ from the dead,

7 Facts about Marriage

CULTURE NOWADAYS WANTS to redefine what marriage is, there are many people nowadays who want to marry the same gender, there are even some cases where people have "married" themselves, and another case where someone claims to have or wants to marry an anime character. Whatever the case may be society doesn't get to decide who gets to marry who because marriage is not a social construct. It was created by God, so he gets to decide the terms.

For this section I just want to list seven facts about matrimony, supported by scripture of course. Elsewhere in this book (the next section, in fact) you can find 20 tips for husbands and wives, to improve the marriage relationship.

1. Marriage is a between a man and a women.

Gen 2:24 Therefore shall a man leave his father and his mother, and shall cleave unto his wife: and they shall be one flesh.

2. It is for life.

Rom 7:2 For the woman which hath an husband is bound by the law to *her* husband so long as he liveth; but if the husband be dead, she is loosed from the law of *her* husband.

Rom 7:3 So then if, while *her* husband liveth, she be married to another man, she shall be called an adulteress: but if her husband be dead, she is free from that law; so that she is no adulteress, though she be married to another man.

3. There is no marriage in the hereafter (saving our marriage to Jesus)

Mat 22:30 For in the resurrection they neither marry, nor are given in marriage, but are as the angels of God in heaven.

4. Polygamy is wrong.

1Co 7:2 Nevertheless, *to avoid* fornication, let every man have his own wife, and let every woman have her own husband.

5. *We are told not to withhold physical intimacy from our spouse.*

1Co 7:5 Defraud ye not one the other, except *it be* with consent for a time, that ye may give yourselves to fasting and prayer; and come together again, that Satan tempt you not for your incontinency.

6. *There is judgment waiting for those who break wedlock.*

Heb 13:4 Marriage *is* honourable in all, and the bed undefiled: but whoremongers and adulterers God will judge.

7. *The church is the bride of Christ.*

2Co 11:2 For I am jealous over you with godly jealousy: for I have espoused you to one husband, that I may present you as a chaste virgin to Christ.

20 Biblical Marriage Tips

EVERYONE'S MARRIAGE has it's ups and downs (or so I would suppose), It can be a challenge living with someone whose way of life or mode of living could be so different that what you are accustomed to. Marriage takes work, compromise, love and commitment.

Here are twenty tips that can greatly improve one's marriage, if followed. This list is not chronological as it would appear in scripture, but rather sorted out by points.

1. Husbands should be good providers (women value security).

Pro 21:20 *There is* treasure to be desired and oil in the dwelling of the wise; but a foolish man spendeth it up.

1Ti 5:8 But if any provide not for his own, and specially for those of his own house, he hath denied the faith, and is worse than an infidel.

2. Women be submissive their husbands.

1Pe 3:1 Likewise, ye wives, *be* in subjection to your own husbands; that, if any obey not the word, they also may without the word be won by the conversation of the wives;

Eph 5:24 Therefore as the church is subject unto Christ, so *let* the wives *be* to their own husbands in every thing.

3. Men cherish your wives and avoid porn.

Pro 5:19 *Let her be as* the loving hind and pleasant roe; let her breasts satisfy thee at all times; and be thou ravished always with her love.

Eph 5:29 For no man ever yet hated his own flesh; but nourisheth and cherisheth it, even as the Lord the church:

4. Don't disrespect in-laws.

2Co 12:20 For I fear, lest, when I come, I shall not find you such as I would, and *that* I shall be found unto you such as ye would not: lest *there be* debates, envyings, wraths, strifes, backbitings, whisperings, swellings, tumults:

Tit 3:2 To speak evil of no man, to be no brawlers, *but* gentle, shewing all meekness unto all men.

5. Husbands get to know your wives.

1Pe 3:7 Likewise, ye husbands, dwell with *them* according to knowledge, giving honour unto the wife, as unto the weaker vessel, and as being heirs together of the grace of life; that your prayers be not hindered.

6. Wives don't nag.

Pro 19:13 A foolish son *is* the calamity of his father: and the contentions of a wife *are* a continual dropping.

Pro 21:19 *It is* better to dwell in the wilderness, than with a contentious and an angry woman.

Pro 27:15 A continual dropping in a very rainy day and a contentious woman are alike.

7. Husbands watch how you speak to your wives.

Pro 12:18 There is that speaketh like the piercings of a sword: but the tongue of the wise *is* health.

Pro 18:21 Death and life *are* in the power of the tongue: and they that love it shall eat the fruit thereof.

8. Husbands pay attention to what she says.

Jas 1:19 Wherefore, my beloved brethren, let every man be swift to hear, slow to speak, slow to wrath:

9. Husbands be good dads and lead the family.

Eph 6:4 And, ye fathers, provoke not your children to wrath: but bring them up in the nurture and admonition of the Lord.

10. Husbands self-sacrificially love your wives.

Eph 5:25 Husbands, love your wives, even as Christ also loved the church, and gave himself for it;

11. Husbands and Wives don't withhold sexual intimacy.

1Co 7:5 Defraud ye not one the other, except *it be* with consent for a time, that ye may give yourselves to fasting and prayer; and come together again, that Satan tempt you not for your incontinency.

12. Husbands forgive your wives, don't hold onto grudges with them.

Col 3:19 Husbands, love *your* wives, and be not bitter against them.

13. Husbands don't make your wife carry 50+% of the workload, women were designed to help not do most of the work.

Gen 2:18 And the LORD God said, *It is* not good that the man should be alone; I will make him an help meet for him.

1Pe 3:7 Likewise, ye husbands, dwell with *them* according to knowledge, giving honour unto the wife, as unto the weaker vessel, and as being heirs together of the grace of life; that your prayers be not hindered.

14. Men be romantic (try telling her how you feel about her poetically)!

Son 4:1 Behold, thou *art* fair, my love; behold, thou *art* fair; thou *hast* doves' eyes within thy locks: thy hair *is* as a flock of goats, that appear from mount Gilead.

Son 4:2 Thy teeth *are* like a flock *of sheep that are even* shorn, which came up from the washing; whereof every one bear twins, and none *is* barren among them.

Son 4:3 Thy lips *are* like a thread of scarlet, and thy speech *is* comely: thy temples *are* like a piece of a pomegranate within thy locks.

15. Avoid gambling, drunkenness, and lust (bad for marriage).

Pro 28:22 He that hasteth to be rich *hath* an evil eye, and considereth not that poverty shall come upon him.

Pro 23:21 For the drunkard and the glutton shall come to poverty: and drowsiness shall clothe *a man* with rags.

Job 31:12 For it *is* a fire *that* consumeth to destruction, and would root out all mine increase.

16. Wives learn to cook healthy food (A healthy body makes life easier)

Psa 103:5 Who satisfieth thy mouth with good *things; so that* thy youth is renewed like the eagle's.

17. Husbands find a good church/friends (for emotional support, plus accountability).

Pro 13:20 He that walketh with wise *men* shall be wise: but a companion of fools shall be destroyed.

Heb 10:25 Not forsaking the assembling of ourselves together, as the manner of some *is;* but exhorting *one another:* and so much the more, as ye see the day approaching.

18. Women learn female skills (sewing, crochet, knitting).

Pro 31:13 She seeketh wool, and flax, and worketh willingly with her hands.

Pro 31:18 She perceiveth that her merchandise *is* good: her candle goeth not out by night.

Pro 31:24 She maketh fine linen, and selleth *it;* and delivereth girdles unto the merchant.

19. Have arguments civil, don't raise voices. Be sympathetic.

1Pe 3:8 Finally, *be ye* all of one mind, having compassion one of another, love as brethren, *be* pitiful, *be* courteous:

1Pe 3:9 Not rendering evil for evil, or railing for railing: but contrariwise blessing; knowing that ye are thereunto called, that ye should inherit a blessing.

20. Have charity toward one another.

1Co 13:4 Charity suffereth long, *and* is kind; charity envieth not; charity vaunteth not itself, is not puffed up,

1Co 13:5 Doth not behave itself unseemly, seeketh not her own, is not easily provoked, thinketh no evil;

1Co 13:6 Rejoiceth not in iniquity, but rejoiceth in the truth;

1Co 13:7 Beareth all things, believeth all things, hopeth all things, endureth all things.

Family Responsibility

IT IS EVERY BELIEVERS duty and privilege to care for their own. We are born into a physical family, and nothing will change the fact of who our brothers, parents, sisters, and cousins are; according to the flesh. For those of us who are blessed enough to be born-again into God's family, we then acquire a much greater extended family in the Spirit, or Spiritual family if you will. This doesn't negate our responsibility to care for our first kin. Indeed 1 Timothy five makes it quite clear that the one who doesn't tend to the needs of his household has denied the faith. So to be clear, we cannot be true disciples of Christ while at the same time neglect to care for those our Heavenly Father has entrusted to us.

Pro 13:22 A good *man* leaveth an inheritance to his children's children: and the wealth of the sinner *is* laid up for the just.

Mar 7:9 And he said unto them, Full well ye reject the commandment of God, that ye may keep your own tradition.

Mar 7:10 For Moses said, Honour thy father and thy mother; and, Whoso curseth father or mother, let him die the death:

Mar 7:11 But ye say, If a man shall say to his father or mother, *It is* Corban, that is to say, a gift, by whatsoever thou mightest be profited by me; *he shall be free.*

Mar 7:12 And ye suffer him no more to do ought for his father or his mother;

Mar 7:13 Making the word of God of none effect through your tradition, which ye have delivered: and many such like things do ye.

Rom 1:31 Without understanding, covenantbreakers, without natural affection, implacable, unmerciful:

Eph 5:25 Husbands, love your wives, even as Christ also loved the church, and gave himself for it;

Eph 6:2 Honour thy father and mother; (which is the first commandment with promise;)

Eph 6:3 That it may be well with thee, and thou mayest live long on the earth.

Eph 6:4 And, ye fathers, provoke not your children to wrath: but bring them up in the nurture and admonition of the Lord.

1Ti 5:4 But if any widow have children or nephews, let them learn first to shew piety at home, and to requite their parents: for that is good and acceptable before God.

1Ti 5:8 But if any provide not for his own, and specially for those of his own house, he hath denied the faith, and is worse than an infidel.

Tit 2:4 That they may teach the young women to be sober, to love their husbands, to love their children,

God Above Family

THIS MAY SEEM LIKE a hard subject to grasp for some. After the bible also teaches to honor and requite your parents, to provide for our own, and for mothers to love their children (though obviously fathers are to love their children as well). Still there must be a priority to our ultimate loyalty. The first commandment of all is Love the Lord your God will all your heart, mind, soul, and strength. To do otherwise would make the family member an idol. Consider that Jesus is the one who gave you your parents and siblings, has never sinned against you, and is the one who blessed you with all of lifes other benefits such as your health, sight, hearing, food, shelter, friends, etc.

To those who would argue that the bible doesn't teach us to Love Jesus more than our earthly kin, take a gander at the verses below. By the way the bible does not teach us to hate our father and mother in the sense that many bible skeptics would suppose. All one has to do is liken that passage in Luke to Matthew 10:37. The point is we are to love Jesus way more than our parents. The whole point is that we shouldn't compromise our morals to please our families.

Just look at the Patriarch Abraham, he is called by scripture the friend of God. We know he was saved. Although we can imagine what kind of inner turmoil went through his mind when he was asked to offer up his son on the alter, still his obedience and determination to put God's will first in this matter made his faith perfect.

GEN 12:1 NOW THE LORD had said unto Abram, Get thee out of thy country, and from thy kindred, and from thy father's house, unto a land that I will shew thee:

Exo 32:27 And he said unto them, Thus saith the LORD God of Israel, Put every man his sword by his side, *and* go in and out from gate to gate throughout the camp, and slay every man his brother, and every man his companion, and every man his neighbour.

Lev 10:6 And Moses said unto Aaron, and unto Eleazar and unto Ithamar, his sons, Uncover not your heads, neither rend your clothes; lest ye die, and lest wrath come upon all the people: but let your brethren, the whole house of Israel, bewail the burning which the LORD hath kindled.

Deu 13:6 If thy brother, the son of thy mother, or thy son, or thy daughter, or the wife of thy bosom, or thy friend, which *is* as thine own soul, entice thee secretly, saying, Let us go and serve other gods, which thou hast not known, thou, nor thy fathers;

Deu 13:8 Thou shalt not consent unto him, nor hearken unto him; neither shall thine eye pity him, neither shalt thou spare, neither shalt thou conceal him:

Deu 13:9 But thou shalt surely kill him; thine hand shall be first upon him to put him to death, and afterwards the hand of all the people.

Mat 8:21 And another of his disciples said unto him, Lord, suffer me first to go and bury my father.

Mat 8:22 But Jesus said unto him, Follow me; and let the dead bury their dead.

Mat 10:34 Think not that I am come to send peace on earth: I came not to send peace, but a sword.

Mat 10:35 For I am come to set a man at variance against his father, and the daughter against her mother, and the daughter in law against her mother in law.

Mat 10:36 And a man's foes *shall be* they of his own household.

Mat 10:37 He that loveth father or mother more than me is not worthy of me: and he that loveth son or daughter more than me is not worthy of me.

Luk 9:61 And another also said, Lord, I will follow thee; but let me first go bid them farewell, which are at home at my house.

Luk 9:62 And Jesus said unto him, No man, having put his hand to the plough, and looking back, is fit for the kingdom of God.

Luk 14:26 If any *man* come to me, and hate not his father, and mother, and wife, and children, and brethren, and sisters, yea, and his own life also, he cannot be my disciple.

1Co 7:29 But this I say, brethren, the time *is* short: it remaineth, that both they that have wives be as though they had none;

Encouraging Verses

WE ALL GO THROUGH TOUGH times in life. Whether it's the death of a loved one, sickness, loss of home or goods, rejection, demonic attacks, divorce, or other causes; life can be hard. Below I have compiled ten sections that deal with various issues that can cause worry or depression. Read some of these when your feeling down, maybe they might cheer you up.

1. Assurance (Doubting Salvation)

Joh 10:29 My Father, which gave *them* me, is greater than all; and no *man* is able to pluck *them* out of my Father's hand.

Rom 5:9 Much more then, being now justified by his blood, we shall be saved from wrath through him.

Rom 5:10 For if, when we were enemies, we were reconciled to God by the death of his Son, much more, being reconciled, we shall be saved by his life.

Eph 2:8 For by grace are ye saved through faith; and that not of yourselves: *it is* the gift of God:

2. Provision (Worrying about Bills, etc)

Mat 6:25 Therefore I say unto you, Take no thought for your life, what ye shall eat, or what ye shall drink; nor yet for your body, what ye shall put on. Is not the life more than meat, and the body than raiment?

Mat 6:26 Behold the fowls of the air: for they sow not, neither do they reap, nor gather into barns; yet your heavenly Father feedeth them. Are ye not much better than they?

Mat 6:30 Wherefore, if God so clothe the grass of the field, which to day is, and to morrow is cast into the oven, *shall he* not much more *clothe* you, O ye of little faith?

Mat 6:31 Therefore take no thought, saying, What shall we eat? or, What shall we drink? or, Wherewithal shall we be clothed?

3. Body Image

1Sa 16:7 But the LORD said unto Samuel, Look not on his countenance, or on the height of his stature; because I have refused him: for *the LORD seeth* not as man seeth; for man looketh on the outward appearance, but the LORD looketh on the heart.

Psa 39:5 Behold, thou hast made my days *as* an handbreadth; and mine age *is* as nothing before thee: verily every man at his best state *is* altogether vanity. Selah.

Pro 31:30 Favour *is* deceitful, and beauty *is* vain: *but* a woman *that* feareth the LORD, she shall be praised.

Isa 45:9 Woe unto him that striveth with his Maker! *Let* the potsherd *strive* with the potsherds of the earth. Shall the clay say to him that fashioneth it, What makest thou? or thy work, He hath no hands?

4. God's Love for You

Rom 8:35 Who shall separate us from the love of Christ? *shall* tribulation, or distress, or persecution, or famine, or nakedness, or peril, or sword?

Rom 8:37 Nay, in all these things we are more than conquerors through him that loved us.

Rom 8:38 For I am persuaded, that neither death, nor life, nor angels, nor principalities, nor powers, nor things present, nor things to come,

Rom 8:39 Nor height, nor depth, nor any other creature, shall be able to separate us from the love of God, which is in Christ Jesus our Lord.

5. Regret

2Co 5:17 Therefore if any man *be* in Christ, *he is* a new creature: old things are passed away; behold, all things are become new.

2Co 7:9 Now I rejoice, not that ye were made sorry, but that ye sorrowed to repentance: for ye were made sorry after a godly manner, that ye might receive damage by us in nothing.

Php 3:13 Brethren, I count not myself to have apprehended: but *this* one thing *I do,* forgetting those things which are behind, and reaching forth unto those things which are before,

6. Courage

Jos 1:9 Have not I commanded thee? Be strong and of a good courage; be not afraid, neither be thou dismayed: for the LORD thy God *is* with thee whithersoever thou goest.

Psa 27:14 Wait on the LORD: be of good courage, and he shall strengthen thine heart: wait, I say, on the LORD.

Mat 10:28 And fear not them which kill the body, but are not able to kill the soul: but rather fear him which is able to destroy both soul and body in hell.

2Ti 1:7 For God hath not given us the spirit of fear; but of power, and of love, and of a sound mind.

7. Trust

Psa 34:22 The LORD redeemeth the soul of his servants: and none of them that trust in him shall be desolate.

Psa 37:3 Trust in the LORD, and do good; *so* shalt thou dwell in the land, and verily thou shalt be fed.

Psa 37:5 Commit thy way unto the LORD; trust also in him; and he shall bring *it* to pass.

1Ti 4:10 For therefore we both labour and suffer reproach, because we trust in the living God, who is the Saviour of all men, specially of those that believe.

8. Circumstances (Housing Issues, Relationship Problems, etc)

Mat 19:26 But Jesus beheld *them,* and said unto them, With men this is impossible; but with God all things are possible.

Rom 8:25 But if we hope for that we see not, *then* do we with patience wait for *it.*

2Co 4:18 While we look not at the things which are seen, but at the things which are not seen: for the things which are seen *are* temporal; but the things which are not seen *are* eternal.

2Co 5:7 (For we walk by faith, not by sight:)

9. Health

Exo_15:26 And said, If thou wilt diligently hearken to the voice of the LORD thy God, and wilt do that which is right in his sight, and wilt give ear to his commandments, and keep all his statutes, I will put none of these diseases upon thee, which I have brought upon the Egyptians: for I *am* the LORD that healeth thee.

Psa 103:3 Who forgiveth all thine iniquities; who healeth all thy diseases;

Psa 147:3 He healeth the broken in heart, and bindeth up their wounds.

Mat 8:16 When the even was come, they brought unto him many that were possessed with devils: and he cast out the spirits with *his* word, and healed all that were sick:

Mat 8:17 That it might be fulfilled which was spoken by Esaias the prophet, saying, Himself took our infirmities, and bare *our* sicknesses.

2Co 12:9 And he said unto me, My grace is sufficient for thee: for my strength is made perfect in weakness. Most gladly therefore will I rather glory in my infirmities, that the power of Christ may rest upon me.

10. General

Isa 40:30 Even the youths shall faint and be weary, and the young men shall utterly fall:

Isa 40:31 But they that wait upon the LORD shall renew *their* strength; they shall mount up with wings as eagles; they shall run, and not be weary; *and* they shall walk, and not faint.

Php 4:13 I can do all things through Christ which strengtheneth me.

Fasting

IF I HAD TO VENTURE a guess, I would assume that fasting is no one's favorite bible topic. Nevertheless fasting is an essential component of the Christian faith. Too many in the church (including myself) has neglected this important aspect of Christianity. I wonder what percentage of the church actually fast. Jesus says when ye fast (Mat 6:16), not if you fast.

So what is the purpose of fasting? For the first part this study I am going to list three quick facts about fasting.

1. From Isaiah we see that one of it's purposes is to bring the flesh into subjection or to put it another way; to loosen sin's hold on us. We can see from the book of Jonah that Nineveh fasted while they repented.

2. From the gospels (Mat 17, Mark 9) we see that fasting is a part of spiritual warfare as certain evil spirits can only be driven out by prayer and fasting, (though given the context, some may point out that it was the lack of faith that made the disciples unable to cast of the evil spirit). Some translations remove fasting from these passages, as well in 1 Corinthians 7.

3. We also see from passages such as 2 Samuel 12, Esther 4, and Daniel 6 that people fast when they are in distress.

For this section I'm going to do this in a Q&A format.

What kinds of Fast are there?

Well the most extreme fast I can think of is Moses when he was with the Lord, he didn't eat bread nor drink water for forty days. Most people would probably die if they didn't drink anything for a few days. I don't think I could ever go to that extreme in fasting nor would I recommend it. Daniel's fast had him eating no pleasant bread, nor flesh/wine, so I assume he ate bland food. He did this for an extended amount of time; the length of which I discuss in the next question. I personally, usually do something like a 1 day water only fast myself.

How Long Can I Fast?

The longest fast according to scripture is a tie between Jesus and Moses at 40 days. Daniel had a 3 week fast, and we see Esther and Mordecai fasted for three days. For one of if not the shortest fast in the bible we have king Saul forcing the people to not eat food until the evening! I would say it is up to the person doing the fast how long they are going to do it for though.

Can you fast from things other than Food?

This issue is debated and this author will give no clear answer. Some Christians argue that you can only fast from food, while others say you can do a TV, Cell phone, or other type of fast. There is one interesting point I would like to make and that is in 1st Corinthians 7 we see that we are supposed to abstain from sex during our fast.

Are there any health risk/benefits associated with fasting?

Sadly, to cover all the health benefits and / or risk of fasting is beyond the scope of this study, however I will just list some of the health benefits/risk briefly here.

Risk/Symptoms Benefits

1. Hunger/Cravings Lower Blood Pressure
2. Irritability Lower Blood Sugar
3. Headaches/Dizziness Improved Brain Health
4. Fatigue Weight Loss
5. Malnutrition Less Inflammation

The information for the previous list was gathered from the following sites: https://www.massgeneralbrigham.org/en/about/newsroom/articles/pros-and-cons-of-intermittent-fasting

https://www.healthline.com/nutrition/intermittent-fasting-side-effects#hunger

Here is just a sample of the verses on fasting.

———————————————

2SA 12:23 BUT NOW he is dead, wherefore should I fast? can I bring him back again? I shall go to him, but he shall not return to me.

2Ch 20:3 And Jehoshaphat feared, and set himself to seek the LORD, and proclaimed a fast throughout all Judah.

Ezr 8:21 Then I proclaimed a fast there, at the river of Ahava, that we might afflict ourselves before our God, to seek of him a right way for us, and for our little ones, and for all our substance.

Est 4:16 Go, gather together all the Jews that are present in Shushan, and fast ye for me, and neither eat nor drink three days, night or day: I also and my maidens will fast likewise; and so will I go in unto the king, which *is* not according to the law: and if I perish, I perish.

Psa 35:13 But as for me, when they were sick, my clothing *was* sackcloth: I humbled my soul with fasting; and my prayer returned into mine own bosom.

Psa 69:10 When I wept, *and chastened* my soul with fasting, that was to my reproach.

Isa 58:3 Wherefore have we fasted, *say they,* and thou seest not? *wherefore* have we afflicted our soul, and thou takest no knowledge? Behold, in the day of your fast ye find pleasure, and exact all your labours.

Isa 58:4 Behold, ye fast for strife and debate, and to smite with the fist of wickedness: ye shall not fast as *ye do this* day, to make your voice to be heard on high.

Isa 58:5 Is it such a fast that I have chosen? a day for a man to afflict his soul? *is it* to bow down his head as a bulrush, and to spread sackcloth and ashes *under him?* wilt thou call this a fast, and an acceptable day to the LORD?

Isa 58:6 *Is* not this the fast that I have chosen? to loose the bands of wickedness, to undo the heavy burdens, and to let the oppressed go free, and that ye break every yoke?

Jer 36:6 Therefore go thou, and read in the roll, which thou hast written from my mouth, the words of the LORD in the ears of the people in the LORD'S house upon the fasting day: and also thou shalt read them in the ears of all Judah that come out of their cities.

Dan 6:18 Then the king went to his palace, and passed the night fasting: neither were instruments of musick brought before him: and his sleep went from him.

Dan 9:3 And I set my face unto the Lord God, to seek by prayer and supplications, with fasting, and sackcloth, and ashes:

Joe 2:12 Therefore also now, saith the LORD, turn ye *even* to me with all your heart, and with fasting, and with weeping, and with mourning:

Jon 3:5 So the people of Nineveh believed God, and proclaimed a fast, and put on sackcloth, from the greatest of them even to the least of them.

Zec 8:19 Thus saith the LORD of hosts; The fast of the fourth *month,* and the fast of the fifth, and the fast of the seventh, and the fast of the tenth, shall be to the house of Judah joy and gladness, and cheerful feasts; therefore love the truth and peace.

Mat 6:16 Moreover when ye fast, be not, as the hypocrites, of a sad countenance: for they disfigure their faces, that they may appear unto men to fast. Verily I say unto you, They have their reward.

Mat 6:17 But thou, when thou fastest, anoint thine head, and wash thy face;

Mat 6:18 That thou appear not unto men to fast, but unto thy Father which is in secret: and thy Father, which seeth in secret, shall reward thee openly.

Mar 9:29 And he said unto them, This kind can come forth by nothing, but by prayer and fasting.

1Co 7:5 Defraud ye not one the other, except *it be* with consent for a time, that ye may give yourselves to fasting and prayer; and come together again, that Satan tempt you not for your incontinency.

Sacrifice

WHAT COMES TO MIND when you think of sacrifice? How about the book of Leviticus, it gives very detailed information on how the Levitical priesthood was to carry out their sacrifices to God. Animal sacrifices were a type of foreshadowing of Jesus' death on the Cross, animal sacrifices could never wash away sins; only the blood of Christ can do that. Only the best animals were to be sacrificed to the Lord, no blemish or evil-favouredness were to be permitted. Although we read from Malachi that the priest's were not following this rule; much to the displeasure of the Lord.

What types of animals where sacrificed under the Old Covenant?

- Lambs

- Goats

- Bullocks

- Pigeons

These are the ones that come to my mind when I think of the old Levitical sacrificial laws, although it's possible I could be forgetting a few. The list of clean and unclean foods are listed in Leviticus 11 as I assume most mature Christians already know. Although just because an animal is on the clean list it doesn't mean the Israelite's were instructed to offer it as a burnt offering. For instance I do not recall roebuck and harts being used as burnt offerings in scripture at all.

If one does a keyword search of the phrase lord shall choose, you should get twenty-six verses pop up (if using the KJV), twenty of which appear in Deuteronomy. The phrase was stated many times in scripture this is in reference to where the Israelite's were to offer their sacrifices. It's in the place the Lord shall choose. Today we are to offer up spiritual sacrifices to God.

With that said the Lord prefers obedience rather than sacrifice. The bible calls us to present our bodies as a living sacrifice to God. We are to desire to do his will rather than our own, for his will is perfect; Jesus surely knows what's best for us. For if we are rebellious to the Lord and do not desire to do his will then what good would sacrifice do us? For the sacrifice of the wicked is an abomination to the Lord.

Deu 15:21 And if there be *any* blemish therein, *as if it be* lame, or blind, *or have* any ill blemish, thou shalt not sacrifice it unto the LORD thy God.

Deu 17:1 Thou shalt not sacrifice unto the LORD thy God *any* bullock, or sheep, wherein is blemish, *or* any evilfavouredness: for that *is* an abomination unto the LORD thy God.

1Sa 15:22 And Samuel said, Hath the LORD *as great* delight in burnt offerings and sacrifices, as in obeying the voice of the LORD? Behold, to obey *is* better than sacrifice, *and* to hearken than the fat of rams.

2Ki 17:35 With whom the LORD had made a covenant, and charged them, saying, Ye shall not fear other gods, nor bow yourselves to them, nor serve them, nor sacrifice to them:

Psa 40:6 Sacrifice and offering thou didst not desire; mine ears hast thou opened: burnt offering and sin offering hast thou not required.

Psa 40:7 Then said I, Lo, I come: in the volume of the book *it is* written of me,

Psa 40:8 I delight to do thy will, O my God: yea, thy law *is* within my heart.

Pro 15:8 The sacrifice of the wicked *is* an abomination to the LORD: but the prayer of the upright *is* his delight.

Isa 1:11 To what purpose *is* the multitude of your sacrifices unto me? saith the LORD: I am full of the burnt offerings of rams, and the fat of fed beasts; and I delight not in the blood of bullocks, or of lambs, or of he goats.

Isa 1:12 When ye come to appear before me, who hath required this at your hand, to tread my courts?

Isa 1:13 Bring no more vain oblations; incense is an abomination unto me; the new moons and sabbaths, the calling of assemblies, I cannot away with; *it is* iniquity, even the solemn meeting.

Hos 6:6 For I desired mercy, and not sacrifice; and the knowledge of God more than burnt offerings.

Mal 1:8 And if ye offer the blind for sacrifice, *is it* not evil? and if ye offer the lame and sick, *is it* not evil? offer it now unto thy governor; will he be pleased with thee, or accept thy person? saith the LORD of hosts.

Rom 12:1 I beseech you therefore, brethren, by the mercies of God, that ye present your bodies a living sacrifice, holy, acceptable unto God, *which is* your reasonable service.

Heb 10:4 For *it is* not possible that the blood of bulls and of goats should take away sins.

Heb 10:5 Wherefore when he cometh into the world, he saith, Sacrifice and offering thou wouldest not, but a body hast thou prepared me:

Heb 10:6 In burnt offerings and *sacrifices* for sin thou hast had no pleasure.

Heb 10:7 Then said I, Lo, I come (in the volume of the book it is written of me,) to do thy will, O God.

Heb 13:15 By him therefore let us offer the sacrifice of praise to God continually, that is, the fruit of *our* lips giving thanks to his name.

1Pe 2:5 Ye also, as lively stones, are built up a spiritual house, an holy priesthood, to offer up spiritual sacrifices, acceptable to God by Jesus Christ.

List of Spiritual Gifts

JUST AS OUR BODIES are comprised of many different members, so too the body of Christ is made up of many members. We see that our earthly bodies have different parts with differing functions; for example, the eye sees, and the nose smells. The church as well has many different functions among it's parts (or people I should say). Some Christians have the gift of teaching, others have a gift of exhortation (or encouragement), some Christians have the ability to speak in other tongues, others have the gift of healing; whatever your gift is, use it for the glory of God and the edifying of the church (1 Cor 10:31, 1 Cor 14, Eph 4).

One difference between Baptists and Pentecostals is the doctrine of cessation-ism vs the doctrine of continuation-ism. Which all boils down to whether not some of the spiritual gifts have ceased or not (namely tongues, interpretation of tongues, healing, and working of miracles). I plan on covering this topic more in depth in my subsequent book, Vol. 3; so there is no need to speak more on it here.

Rom 12:6 Having then gifts differing according to the grace that is given to us, whether prophecy, *let us prophesy* according to the proportion of faith;

Rom 12:7 Or ministry, *let us wait* on *our* ministering: or he that teacheth, on teaching;

Rom 12:8 Or he that exhorteth, on exhortation: he that giveth, *let him do it* with simplicity; he that ruleth, with diligence; he that sheweth mercy, with cheerfulness.

1Co 12:8 For to one is given by the Spirit the word of wisdom; to another the word of knowledge by the same Spirit;

1Co 12:9 To another faith by the same Spirit; to another the gifts of healing by the same Spirit;

1Co 12:10 To another the working of miracles; to another prophecy; to another discerning of spirits; to another *divers* kinds of tongues; to another the interpretation of tongues:

1Co 12:11 But all these worketh that one and the selfsame Spirit, dividing to every man severally as he will.

1Co 12:28 And God hath set some in the church, first apostles, secondarily prophets, thirdly teachers, after that miracles, then gifts of healings, helps, governments, diversities of tongues.

Eph 4:11 And he gave some, apostles; and some, prophets; and some, evangelists; and some, pastors and teachers;

The word of God

FIRST SOME BASIC FACTS about the bible. The bible is not one book, it is a collection of 66 books. It was written by 40 men over the coarse of 2000 years (Approximately). It was originally written in three languages, (Hebrew, Aramaic, and Greek). The authors came from many different walks of life, such as shepherd, fisherman, a cup-bearer, kings, prophets, and more. Despite the differences in occupation the bible's message remains the same. God made the world, it was flooded, Christ Died for the sins of the world, and there will be a judgment day.

Now some spiritual truths about the scriptures. The bible tells us that...

- man lives by the word of God

- the word is truth and we are sanctified by truth

- the word washes us

- faith comes by hearing the word

- the word is likened to milk, it is for our spritual growth

- Jesus is the Living Word

The word of God is to be valued above rubies and gold, it is a light unto our feet. If you desire to be blessed, consider Psalm 1, it shows us how one can be blessed; by delighting in and meditating on God's word. There is a common acronym for the (B.I.B.L.E) it is *basic instructions before leaving earth*. Two of the most important aspects of a Christians walk are prayer and reading/applying the word of God. Consider Psalm 119:11 "Thy word have I hid in mine heart, that I might not sin against thee".

Since there are so many verses listed in this study, why don't I go ahead a break this down into a few or several sections for easy lookup.

CATEGORY #1: PRESERVATION of the word.

Deu 30:12 It *is* not in heaven, that thou shouldest say, Who shall go up for us to heaven, and bring it unto us, that we may hear it, and do it?

Deu 30:13 Neither *is* it beyond the sea, that thou shouldest say, Who shall go over the sea for us, and bring it unto us, that we may hear it, and do it?

Deu 30:14 But the word *is* very nigh unto thee, in thy mouth, and in thy heart, that thou mayest do it.

Psa 12:6 The words of the LORD *are* pure words: *as* silver tried in a furnace of earth, purified seven times.

Psa 12:7 Thou shalt keep them, O LORD, thou shalt preserve them from this generation for ever.

Psa 100:5 For the LORD *is* good; his mercy *is* everlasting; and his truth *endureth* to all generations.

Psa 119:160 Thy word *is* true *from* the beginning: and every one of thy righteous judgments *endureth* for ever.

Isa 59:21 As for me, this *is* my covenant with them, saith the LORD; My spirit that *is* upon thee, and my words which I have put in thy mouth, shall not depart out of thy mouth, nor out of the mouth of thy seed, nor out of the mouth of thy seed's seed, saith the LORD, from henceforth and for ever.

Mar 13:31 Heaven and earth shall pass away: but my words shall not pass away.

Joh 10:35 If he called them gods, unto whom the word of God came, and the scripture cannot be broken;

1Pe 1:23 Being born again, not of corruptible seed, but of incorruptible, by the word of God, which liveth and abideth for ever.

1Pe 1:24 For all flesh *is* as grass, and all the glory of man as the flower of grass. The grass withereth, and the flower thereof falleth away:

1Pe 1:25 But the word of the Lord endureth for ever. And this is the word which by the gospel is preached unto you.

Category #2: Value of the word.

Job 23:12 Neither have I gone back from the commandment of his lips; I have esteemed the words of his mouth more than my necessary *food*.

Psa 19:10 More to be desired *are they* than gold, yea, than much fine gold: sweeter also than honey and the honeycomb.

Psa 119:72 The law of thy mouth *is* better unto me than thousands of gold and silver.

Category #3: It's spiritual functions.

Psa 19:7 The law of the LORD *is* perfect, converting the soul: the testimony of the LORD *is* sure, making wise the simple.

Psa 19:8 The statutes of the LORD *are* right, rejoicing the heart: the commandment of the LORD *is* pure, enlightening the eyes.

Psa 19:9 The fear of the LORD *is* clean, enduring for ever: the judgments of the LORD *are* true *and* righteous altogether.

Psa 19:11 Moreover by them is thy servant warned: *and* in keeping of them *there is* great reward.

Psa 119:50 This *is* my comfort in my affliction: for thy word hath quickened me.

Psa 119:93 I will never forget thy precepts: for with them thou hast quickened me.

Jer 23:29 *Is* not my word like as a fire? saith the LORD; and like a hammer *that* breaketh the rock in pieces?

Joh 17:17 Sanctify them through thy truth: thy word is truth.

Rom 10:17 So then faith *cometh* by hearing, and hearing by the word of God.

Eph 1:13 In whom ye also *trusted,* after that ye heard the word of truth, the gospel of your salvation: in whom also after that ye believed, ye were sealed with that holy Spirit of promise,

Eph 5:26 That he might sanctify and cleanse it with the washing of water by the word,

2Ti 3:15 And that from a child thou hast known the holy scriptures, which are able to make thee wise unto salvation through faith which is in Christ Jesus.

Jas 1:21 Wherefore lay apart all filthiness and superfluity of naughtiness, and receive with meekness the engrafted word, which is able to save your souls.

1Pe 2:2 As newborn babes, desire the sincere milk of the word, that ye may grow thereby:

Category #4: Better obey it.

Lev 18:26 Ye shall therefore keep my statutes and my judgments, and shall not commit *any* of these abominations; *neither* any of your own nation, nor any stranger that sojourneth among you:

Num 15:31 Because he hath despised the word of the LORD, and hath broken his commandment, that soul shall utterly be cut off; his iniquity *shall be* upon him.

Deu 8:3 And he humbled thee, and suffered thee to hunger, and fed thee with manna, which thou knewest not, neither did thy fathers know; that he might make thee know that man doth not live by bread only, but by every *word* that proceedeth out of the mouth of the LORD doth man live.

Psa 119:9 BETH. Wherewithal shall a young man cleanse his way? by taking heed *thereto* according to thy word.

Psa 119:11 Thy word have I hid in mine heart, that I might not sin against thee.

Mat 4:4 But he answered and said, It is written, Man shall not live by bread alone, but by every word that proceedeth out of the mouth of God.

Mat 7:24 Therefore whosoever heareth these sayings of mine, and doeth them, I will liken him unto a wise man, which built his house upon a rock:

Joh 14:23 Jesus answered and said unto him, If a man love me, he will keep my words: and my Father will love him, and we will come unto him, and make our abode with him.

Jas 1:22 But be ye doers of the word, and not hearers only, deceiving your own selves.

Jas 1:23 For if any be a hearer of the word, and not a doer, he is like unto a man beholding his natural face in a glass:

Jas 1:24 For he beholdeth himself, and goeth his way, and straightway forgetteth what manner of man he was.

Jas 1:25 But whoso looketh into the perfect law of liberty, and continueth *therein,* he being not a forgetful hearer, but a doer of the work, this man shall be blessed in his deed.

1Jn 2:3 And hereby we do know that we know him, if we keep his commandments.

1Jn 2:4 He that saith, I know him, and keepeth not his commandments, is a liar, and the truth is not in him.

1Jn 2:5 But whoso keepeth his word, in him verily is the love of God perfected: hereby know we that we are in him.

1Jn 5:3 For this is the love of God, that we keep his commandments: and his commandments are not grievous.

Category # 5: Do not add, take, or change the word.

Deu 4:2 Ye shall not add unto the word which I command you, neither shall ye diminish *ought* from it, that ye may keep the commandments of the LORD your God which I command you.

Pro 30:6 Add thou not unto his words, lest he reprove thee, and thou be found a liar.

Jer 23:30 Therefore, behold, I *am* against the prophets, saith the LORD, that steal my words every one from his neighbour.

Jer 23:36 And the burden of the LORD shall ye mention no more: for every man's word shall be his burden; for ye have perverted the words of the living God, of the LORD of hosts our God.

2Co 2:17 For we are not as many, which corrupt the word of God: but as of sincerity, but as of God, in the sight of God speak we in Christ.

2Pe 3:16 As also in all *his* epistles, speaking in them of these things; in which are some things hard to be understood, which they that are unlearned and unstable wrest, as *they do* also the other scriptures, unto their own destruction.

Rev 22:18 For I testify unto every man that heareth the words of the prophecy of this book, If any man shall add unto these things, God shall add unto him the plagues that are written in this book:

Rev 22:19 And if any man shall take away from the words of the book of this prophecy, God shall take away his part out of the book of life, and out of the holy city, and *from* the things which are written in this book.

Category #6: Search, Study, and Meditate.

Psa 1:1 Blessed *is* the man that walketh not in the counsel of the ungodly, nor standeth in the way of sinners, nor sitteth in the seat of the scornful.

Psa 1:2 But his delight *is* in the law of the LORD; and in his law doth he meditate day and night.

Psa 1:3 And he shall be like a tree planted by the rivers of water, that bringeth forth his fruit in his season; his leaf also shall not wither; and whatsoever he doeth shall prosper.

Psa 119:48 My hands also will I lift up unto thy commandments, which I have loved; and I will meditate in thy statutes.

Psa 119:97 MEM. O how love I thy law! it *is* my meditation all the day.

Psa 119:99 I have more understanding than all my teachers: for thy testimonies *are* my meditation.

Isa 34:16 Seek ye out of the book of the LORD, and read: no one of these shall fail, none shall want her mate: for my mouth it hath commanded, and his spirit it hath gathered them.

Joh 5:39 Search the scriptures; for in them ye think ye have eternal life: and they are they which testify of me.

Act 17:11 These were more noble than those in Thessalonica, in that they received the word with all readiness of mind, and searched the scriptures daily, whether those things were so.

Ti 2:15 Study to shew thyself approved unto God, a workman that needeth not to be ashamed, rightly dividing the word of truth.

Category #7: Inspiration

1Th 2:13 For this cause also thank we God without ceasing, because, when ye received the word of God which ye heard of us, ye received *it* not *as* the word of men, but as it is in truth, the word of God, which effectually worketh also in you that believe.

2Ti 3:16 All scripture *is* given by inspiration of God, and *is* profitable for doctrine, for reproof, for correction, for instruction in righteousness:

2Pe 1:19 We have also a more sure word of prophecy; whereunto ye do well that ye take heed, as unto a light that shineth in a dark place, until the day dawn, and the day star arise in your hearts:

2Pe 1:20 Knowing this first, that no prophecy of the scripture is of any private interpretation.

2Pe 1:21 For the prophecy came not in old time by the will of man: but holy men of God spake *as they were* moved by the Holy Ghost.

Category #8: Other

Gen 15:1 After these things the word of the LORD came unto Abram in a vision, saying, Fear not, Abram: I *am* thy shield, *and* thy exceeding great reward.

2Sa 24:11 For when David was up in the morning, the word of the LORD came unto the prophet Gad, David's seer, saying,

1Ki 13:1 And, behold, there came a man of God out of Judah by the word of the LORD unto Bethel: and Jeroboam stood by the altar to burn incense.

2Ch 36:21 To fulfil the word of the LORD by the mouth of Jeremiah, until the land had enjoyed her sabbaths: *for* as long as she lay desolate she kept sabbath, to fulfil threescore and ten years.

1Sa 9:27 *And* as they were going down to the end of the city, Samuel said to Saul, Bid the servant pass on before us, (and he passed on,) but stand thou still a while, that I may shew thee the word of God.

Deu 27:8 And thou shalt write upon the stones all the words of this law very plainly.

Deu 29:29 The secret *things belong* unto the LORD our God: but those *things which are* revealed *belong* unto us and to our children for ever, that *we* may do all the words of this law.

Deu 30:11 For this commandment which I command thee this day, it *is* not hidden from thee, neither *is* it far off.

1Sa 3:1 And the child Samuel ministered unto the LORD before Eli. And the word of the LORD was precious in those days; *there was* no open vision.

1Sa 15:23 For rebellion *is as* the sin of witchcraft, and stubbornness *is as* iniquity and idolatry. Because thou hast rejected the word of the LORD, he hath also rejected thee from *being* king.

1Ki 8:56 Blessed *be* the LORD, that hath given rest unto his people Israel, according to all that he promised: there hath not failed one word of all his good promise, which he promised by the hand of Moses his servant.

1Ki 13:2 And he cried against the altar in the word of the LORD, and said, O altar, altar, thus saith the LORD; Behold, a child shall be born unto the house of David, Josiah by name; and upon thee shall he offer the priests of the high places that burn incense upon thee, and men's bones shall be burnt upon thee.

1Ki 17:16 *And* the barrel of meal wasted not, neither did the cruse of oil fail, according to the word of the LORD, which he spake by Elijah.

2Ki 9:36 Wherefore they came again, and told him. And he said, This *is* the word of the LORD, which he spake by his servant Elijah the Tishbite, saying, In the portion of Jezreel shall dogs eat the flesh of Jezebel:

Psa 33:4 For the word of the LORD *is* right; and all his works *are done* in truth.

Psa 56:4 In God I will praise his word, in God I have put my trust; I will not fear what flesh can do unto me.

Psa 119:24 Thy testimonies also *are* my delight *and* my counsellors.

sa 119:36 Incline my heart unto thy testimonies, and not to covetousness.

Psa 119:92 Unless thy law *had been* my delights, I should then have perished in mine affliction.

Psa 119:103 How sweet are thy words unto my taste! *yea, sweeter* than honey to my mouth!

Psa 119:113 SAMECH. I hate *vain* thoughts: but thy law do I love.

Psa 119:136 Rivers of waters run down mine eyes, because they keep not thy law.

Psa 119:140 Thy word *is* very pure: therefore thy servant loveth it.

Psa 119:141 I *am* small and despised: *yet* do not I forget thy precepts.

Psa_138:2 I will worship toward thy holy temple, and praise thy name for thy lovingkindness and for thy truth: for thou hast magnified thy word above all thy name.

Pro 30:5 Every word of God *is* pure: he *is* a shield unto them that put their trust in him.

Isa 28:13 But the word of the LORD was unto them precept upon precept, precept upon precept; line upon line, line upon line; here a little, *and* there a little; that they might go, and fall backward, and be broken, and snared, and taken.

Jer 8:8 How do ye say, We *are* wise, and the law of the LORD *is* with us? Lo, certainly in vain made he *it;* the pen of the scribes *is* in vain.

Jer 8:9 The wise *men* are ashamed, they are dismayed and taken: lo, they have rejected the word of the LORD; and what wisdom *is* in them?

Jer 20:9 Then I said, I will not make mention of him, nor speak any more in his name. But *his word* was in mine heart as a burning fire shut up in my bones, and I was weary with forbearing, and I could not *stay.*

Jon 3:3 So Jonah arose, and went unto Nineveh, according to the word of the LORD. Now Nineveh was an exceeding great city of three days' journey.

Hos 4:1 Hear the word of the LORD, ye children of Israel: for the LORD hath a controversy with the inhabitants of the land, because *there is* no truth, nor mercy, nor knowledge of God in the land.

Amo 8:12 And they shall wander from sea to sea, and from the north even to the east, they shall run to and fro to seek the word of the LORD, and shall not find *it.*

Zec 4:6 Then he answered and spake unto me, saying, This *is* the word of the LORD unto Zerubbabel, saying, Not by might, nor by power, but by my spirit, saith the LORD of hosts.

Mar 7:13 Making the word of God of none effect through your tradition, which ye have delivered: and many such like things do ye.

Luk 8:11 Now the parable is this: The seed is the word of God.

Luk 8:21 And he answered and said unto them, My mother and my brethren are these which hear the word of God, and do it.

Luk 24:27 And beginning at Moses and all the prophets, he expounded unto them in all the scriptures the things concerning himself.

Luk 24:45 Then opened he their understanding, that they might understand the scriptures,

Act 1:16 Men *and* brethren, this scripture must needs have been fulfilled, which the Holy Ghost by the mouth of David spake before concerning Judas, which was guide to them that took Jesus.

Act 18:24 And a certain Jew named Apollos, born at Alexandria, an eloquent man, *and* mighty in the scriptures, came to Ephesus.

Act 18:28 For he mightily convinced the Jews, *and that* publickly, shewing by the scriptures that Jesus was Christ.

1Co 2:14 But the natural man receiveth not the things of the Spirit of God: for they are foolishness unto him: neither can he know *them,* because they are spiritually discerned.

Gal 3:8 And the scripture, foreseeing that God would justify the heathen through faith, preached before the gospel unto Abraham, *saying,* In thee shall all nations be blessed.

Php 2:16 Holding forth the word of life; that I may rejoice in the day of Christ, that I have not run in vain, neither laboured in vain.

Heb 4:12 For the word of God *is* quick, and powerful, and sharper than any twoedged sword, piercing even to the dividing asunder of soul and spirit, and of the joints and marrow, and *is* a discerner of the thoughts and intents of the heart.

Heb 5:13 For every one that useth milk *is* unskilful in the word of righteousness: for he is a babe.

Heb 5:14 But strong meat belongeth to them that are of full age, *even* those who by reason of use have their senses exercised to discern both good and evil.

Knowledge

KNOWLEDGE IN MY OPINION is the first step in the learning process. 2+2=4, that is knowledge. The skill you use to apply said knowledge, that is wisdom. For instance, you take that knowledge of addition and other mathematical equations and apply that to measuring, cutting, and building with lumber. In other words wisdom is the right application of knowledge. The bible says that the fear of the Lord is the beginning of knowledge, and that God's people are destroyed for a lack of knowledge. We learn also that the fall was caused by the eating of the fruit from the tree of knowledge of good and evil; in that sense, the gaining of that knowledge was evil because Adam and Eve lost their childlike innocence and were now culpable for sin.

Knowledge can be dangerous though. That is because of pride. The bible says knowledge puffeth up, we can become very arrogant when we learn a great deal of information. We can get this sense of superiority over others, and we can deceive ourselves into thinking that we are better than others. This pride will separate us from our maker if left unchecked. For God resisteth the proud but gives grace to the humble. Each of us have our own skill sets / strengths & weaknesses. You may be a master of theology but how good are you at building space shuttles. Someone might be good at nutrition, but can't drive a train. The point is stay humble no matter how much you grow.

Gen 2:17 But of the tree of the knowledge of good and evil, thou shalt not eat of it: for in the day that thou eatest thereof thou shalt surely die.

Lev 4:28 Or if his sin, which he hath sinned, come to his knowledge: then he shall bring his offering, a kid of the goats, a female without blemish, for his sin which he hath sinned.

Deu 1:39 Moreover your little ones, which ye said should be a prey, and your children, which in that day had no knowledge between good and evil, they shall go in thither, and unto them will I give it, and they shall possess it.

1Sa 2:3 Talk no more so exceeding proudly; let *not* arrogancy come out of your mouth: for the LORD *is* a God of knowledge, and by him actions are weighed.

Job 21:22 Shall *any* teach God knowledge? seeing he judgeth those that are high.

Job 38:2 Who *is* this that darkeneth counsel by words without knowledge?

Psa 14:4 Have all the workers of iniquity no knowledge? who eat up my people *as* they eat bread, and call not upon the LORD.

Psa 19:2 Day unto day uttereth speech, and night unto night sheweth knowledge.

Psa 119:66 Teach me good judgment and knowledge: for I have believed thy commandments.

Psa 139:6 *Such* knowledge *is* too wonderful for me; it is high, I cannot *attain* unto it.

Psa 144:3 LORD, what *is* man, that thou takest knowledge of him! *or* the son of man, that thou makest account of him!

Pro 1:7 The fear of the LORD *is* the beginning of knowledge: *but* fools despise wisdom and instruction.

Pro 1:22 How long, ye simple ones, will ye love simplicity? and the scorners delight in their scorning, and fools hate knowledge?

Pro 8:10 Receive my instruction, and not silver; and knowledge rather than choice gold.

Pro 8:12 I wisdom dwell with prudence, and find out knowledge of witty inventions.

Pro 10:14 Wise *men* lay up knowledge: but the mouth of the foolish *is* near destruction.

Pro 15:2 The tongue of the wise useth knowledge aright: but the mouth of fools poureth out foolishness.

Pro 18:15 The heart of the prudent getteth knowledge; and the ear of the wise seeketh knowledge.

Pro 19:2 Also, *that* the soul *be* without knowledge, *it is* not good; and he that hasteth with *his* feet sinneth.

Pro 24:5 A wise man *is* strong; yea, a man of knowledge increaseth strength.

Ecc 2:21 For there is a man whose labour *is* in wisdom, and in knowledge, and in equity; yet to a man that hath not laboured therein shall he leave it *for* his portion. This also *is* vanity and a great evil.

Isa 5:13 Therefore my people are gone into captivity, because *they have* no knowledge: and their honourable men *are* famished, and their multitude dried up with thirst.

Isa 28:9 Whom shall he teach knowledge? and whom shall he make to understand doctrine? *them that are* weaned from the milk, *and* drawn from the breasts.

Isa 33:6 And wisdom and knowledge shall be the stability of thy times, *and* strength of salvation: the fear of the LORD *is* his treasure.

Isa 44:25 That frustrateth the tokens of the liars, and maketh diviners mad; that turneth wise *men* backward, and maketh their knowledge foolish;

Jer 3:15 And I will give you pastors according to mine heart, which shall feed you with knowledge and understanding.

Dan 1:17 As for these four children, God gave them knowledge and skill in all learning and wisdom: and Daniel had understanding in all visions and dreams.

Hos 4:6 My people are destroyed for lack of knowledge: because thou hast rejected knowledge, I will also reject thee, that thou shalt be no priest to me: seeing thou hast forgotten the law of thy God, I will also forget thy children.

Hab 2:14 For the earth shall be filled with the knowledge of the glory of the LORD, as the waters cover the sea.

Mal 2:7 For the priest's lips should keep knowledge, and they should seek the law at his mouth: for he *is* the messenger of the LORD of hosts.

Luk 11:52 Woe unto you, lawyers! for ye have taken away the key of knowledge: ye entered not in yourselves, and them that were entering in ye hindered.

Rom 1:28 And even as they did not like to retain God in *their* knowledge, God gave them over to a reprobate mind, to do those things which are not convenient;

Rom 11:33 O the depth of the riches both of the wisdom and knowledge of God! how unsearchable *are* his judgments, and his ways past finding out!

Rom 15:14 And I myself also am persuaded of you, my brethren, that ye also are full of goodness, filled with all knowledge, able also to admonish one another.

1Co 1:5 That in every thing ye are enriched by him, in all utterance, and *in* all knowledge;

1Co 8:1 Now as touching things offered unto idols, we know that we all have knowledge. Knowledge puffeth up, but charity edifieth.

1Co 15:34 Awake to righteousness, and sin not; for some have not the knowledge of God: I speak *this* to your shame.

Eph 3:19 And to know the love of Christ, which passeth knowledge, that ye might be filled with all the fulness of God.

Php 3:8 Yea doubtless, and I count all things *but* loss for the excellency of the knowledge of Christ Jesus my Lord: for whom I have suffered the loss of all things, and do count them *but* dung, that I may win Christ,

Wisdom

WHAT DOES THE BIBLE say about wisdom? It is better than rubies, and gold. It is a defense, and gives life to those that have it. Not once, not twice, but three times is the fear of the Lord said to be the beginning of wisdom or said to be wisdom (Job 28:28, Psalms 111:10, Proverbs 9:10). It is the Lord that gives wisdom, and scripture says we won't be upbraided for asking for it. We are also told not to glory in our wisdom.

James informs us that there is a wisdom from above and there is a wisdom from beneath. As Christians we are to yearn for the wisdom that is from above, that is from God. There is a wisdom of this world, if one wishes to learn about what the bible says about the wisdom of the world, please refer to the verses taken from 1 Corinthians chapters 1 through 3 below.

Here is another excerpt from Websters Revised Abridged Dictionary 1913, "Wis"dom (-dŭm), n. [AS. wīsdōm. See Wise, a., and - dom.]

1. The quality of being wise; knowledge, and the capacity to make due use of it; knowledge of the best ends and the best means; discernment and judgment; discretion; sagacity; skill; dexterity..."

Indeed wisdom is good and can open up wealth building opportunities, however not all wealth building opportunities are good. Scripture says for us to be wise to that which is good and simple concerning evil (Romans 16:19), this may not be an exact quote though. For instance although Pharmacist, Collage Science Professors, and Hollywood Cinematographers probably make bank, there isn't an amount high enough for me to consider doing these occupations. For ease of reference, I will go ahead and sort the topic of wisdom into a few subcategories;

Wisdom as a gift from God.

Exo 28:3 And thou shalt speak unto all *that are* wise hearted, whom I have filled with the spirit of wisdom, that they may make Aaron's garments to consecrate him, that he may minister unto me in the priest's office.

Exo 35:35 Them hath he filled with wisdom of heart, to work all manner of work, of the engraver, and of the cunning workman, and of the embroiderer, in blue, and in purple, in scarlet, and in fine linen, and of the weaver, *even* of them that do any work, and of those that devise cunning work.

Job 38:36 Who hath put wisdom in the inward parts? or who hath given understanding to the heart?

Job 39:17 Because God hath deprived her of wisdom, neither hath he imparted to her understanding.

1Ki 4:29 And God gave Solomon wisdom and understanding exceeding much, and largeness of heart, even as the sand that *is* on the sea shore.

1Ki 4:30 And Solomon's wisdom excelled the wisdom of all the children of the east country, and all the wisdom of Egypt.

1Ki 10:23 So king Solomon exceeded all the kings of the earth for riches and for wisdom.

1Ki 10:24 And all the earth sought to Solomon, to hear his wisdom, which God had put in his heart.

2Ch 1:12 Wisdom and knowledge *is* granted unto thee; and I will give thee riches, and wealth, and honour, such as none of the kings have had that *have been* before thee, neither shall there any after thee have the like.

Pro 2:6 For the LORD giveth wisdom: out of his mouth *cometh* knowledge and understanding.

Pro 2:7 He layeth up sound wisdom for the righteous: *he is* a buckler to them that walk uprightly.

Ecc 2:26 For *God* giveth to a man that *is* good in his sight wisdom, and knowledge, and joy: but to the sinner he giveth travail, to gather and to heap up, that he may give to *him that is* good before God. This also *is* vanity and vexation of spirit.

Luk 21:15 For I will give you a mouth and wisdom, which all your adversaries shall not be able to gainsay nor resist.

Jas 1:5 If any of you lack wisdom, let him ask of God, that giveth to all *men* liberally, and upbraideth not; and it shall be given him.

It's Value.

Job 28:18 No mention shall be made of coral, or of pearls: for the price of wisdom *is* above rubies.

Pro 8:11 For wisdom *is* better than rubies; and all the things that may be desired are not to be compared to it.

Pro 10:21 The lips of the righteous feed many: but fools die for want of wisdom.

Pro 16:16 How much better *is it* to get wisdom than gold! and to get understanding rather to be chosen than silver!

Ecc 7:12 For wisdom *is* a defence, *and* money *is* a defence: but the excellency of knowledge *is, that* wisdom giveth life to them that have it.

Ecc 9:16 Then said I, Wisdom *is* better than strength: nevertheless the poor man's wisdom *is* despised, and his words are not heard.

Downside of wisdom and / or earthly wisdom, etc.

Ecc 1:17 And I gave my heart to know wisdom, and to know madness and folly: I perceived that this also is vexation of spirit.

Ecc 1:18 For in much wisdom *is* much grief: and he that increaseth knowledge increaseth sorrow.

Isa 47:10 For thou hast trusted in thy wickedness: thou hast said, None seeth me. Thy wisdom and thy knowledge, it hath perverted thee; and thou hast said in thine heart, I *am,* and none else beside me.

1Co 1:19 For it is written, I will destroy the wisdom of the wise, and will bring to nothing the understanding of the prudent.

1Co 1:20 Where *is* the wise? where *is* the scribe? where *is* the disputer of this world? hath not God made foolish the wisdom of this world?

1Co 1:21 For after that in the wisdom of God the world by wisdom knew not God, it pleased God by the foolishness of preaching to save them that believe.

1Co 2:4 And my speech and my preaching *was* not with enticing words of man's wisdom, but in demonstration of the Spirit and of power:

1Co 2:5 That your faith should not stand in the wisdom of men, but in the power of God.

1Co 2:6 Howbeit we speak wisdom among them that are perfect: yet not the wisdom of this world, nor of the princes of this world, that come to nought:

1Co 3:19 For the wisdom of this world is foolishness with God. For it is written, He taketh the wise in their own craftiness.

Jas 3:14 But if ye have bitter envying and strife in your hearts, glory not, and lie not against the truth.

Jas 3:15 This wisdom descendeth not from above, but *is* earthly, sensual, devilish.

Jas 3:16 For where envying and strife *is,* there *is* confusion and every evil work.

OTHER/MORE VERSES.

Exo 35:26 And all the women whose heart stirred them up in wisdom spun goats' *hair.*

Job 39:26 Doth the hawk fly by thy wisdom, *and* stretch her wings toward the south?

Psa 90:12 So teach *us* to number our days, that we may apply *our* hearts unto wisdom.

Psa 104:24 O LORD, how manifold are thy works! in wisdom hast thou made them all: the earth is full of thy riches.

Pro 4:7 Wisdom *is* the principal thing; *therefore* get wisdom: and with all thy getting get understanding.

Pro 8:12 I wisdom dwell with prudence, and find out knowledge of witty inventions.

Pro 9:10 The fear of the LORD *is* the beginning of wisdom: and the knowledge of the holy *is* understanding.

Pro 15:21 Folly *is* joy to *him that is* destitute of wisdom: but a man of understanding walketh uprightly.

Pro 17:16 Wherefore *is there* a price in the hand of a fool to get wisdom, seeing *he hath* no heart *to it?*

Pro 17:24 Wisdom *is* before him that hath understanding; but the eyes of a fool *are* in the ends of the earth.

Pro 18:1 Through desire a man, having separated himself, seeketh *and* intermeddleth with all wisdom.

Pro 19:8 He that getteth wisdom loveth his own soul: he that keepeth understanding shall find good.

Pro 21:30 *There is* no wisdom nor understanding nor counsel against the LORD.

Pro 29:3 Whoso loveth wisdom rejoiceth his father: but he that keepeth company with harlots spendeth *his* substance.

Ecc 2:13 Then I saw that wisdom excelleth folly, as far as light excelleth darkness.

Ecc 7:11 Wisdom *is* good with an inheritance: and *by it there is* profit to them that see the sun.

Isa 11:2 And the spirit of the LORD shall rest upon him, the spirit of wisdom and understanding, the spirit of counsel and might, the spirit of knowledge and of the fear of the LORD;

Isa 29:14 Therefore, behold, I will proceed to do a marvellous work among this people, *even* a marvellous work and a wonder: for the wisdom of their wise *men* shall perish, and the understanding of their prudent *men* shall be hid.

Jer 8:9 The wise *men* are ashamed, they are dismayed and taken: lo, they have rejected the word of the LORD; and what wisdom *is* in them?

Jer 9:23 Thus saith the LORD, Let not the wise *man* glory in his wisdom, neither let the mighty *man* glory in his might, let not the rich *man* glory in his riches:

Dan 1:4 Children in whom *was* no blemish, but well favoured, and skilful in all wisdom, and cunning in knowledge, and understanding science, and such as *had* ability in them to stand in the king's palace, and whom they might teach the learning and the tongue of the Chaldeans.

Mar 6:2 And when the sabbath day was come, he began to teach in the synagogue: and many hearing *him* were astonished, saying, From whence hath this *man* these things? and what wisdom *is* this which is given unto him, that even such mighty works are wrought by his hands?

Luk 1:17 And he shall go before him in the spirit and power of Elias, to turn the hearts of the fathers to the children, and the disobedient to the wisdom of the just; to make ready a people prepared for the Lord.

Luk 2:40 And the child grew, and waxed strong in spirit, filled with wisdom: and the grace of God was upon him.

Luk 2:52 And Jesus increased in wisdom and stature, and in favour with God and man.

Luk 7:35 But wisdom is justified of all her children.

1Co 1:22 For the Jews require a sign, and the Greeks seek after wisdom:

1Co 1:24 But unto them which are called, both Jews and Greeks, Christ the power of God, and the wisdom of God.

1Co 2:7 But we speak the wisdom of God in a mystery, *even* the hidden *wisdom,* which God ordained before the world unto our glory:

1Co 2:13 Which things also we speak, not in the words which man's wisdom teacheth, but which the Holy Ghost teacheth; comparing spiritual things with spiritual.

Col 1:28 Whom we preach, warning every man, and teaching every man in all wisdom; that we may present every man perfect in Christ Jesus:

Col 2:3 In whom are hid all the treasures of wisdom and knowledge.

Jas 3:13 Who *is* a wise man and endued with knowledge among you? let him shew out of a good conversation his works with meekness of wisdom.

Jas 3:17 But the wisdom that is from above is first pure, then peaceable, gentle, *and* easy to be intreated, full of mercy and good fruits, without partiality, and without hypocrisy.

Understanding

I'D LIKE TO LIST TWO definitions of the word understanding as follows "1. The act of one who understands a thing, in any sense of the verb; knowledge; discernment; comprehension; interpretation; explanation..."

and

"...3. The power to understand; the intellectual faculty; the intelligence; the rational powers collectively conceived an designated; the higher capacities of the intellect; the power to distinguish truth from falsehood, and to adapt means to ends..." -Websters Revised Unabridged Dictionary 1913

The bible contains all kinds of knowledge, that is, information. It is the Spirit that gives understanding. It is a lack of understanding that is the cause of many a great heresy, or put another way; When we interpret the scripture wrongly this leads to false doctrine.

Some examples of *incorrect* Understanding of Scripture include...

· Supposing Malachi 4:1 teaches Annihilation-ism

· Assuming the baptism of Mark 16:16 means water baptism, endorsing Baptismal Regeneration.

· Claiming that the rich man and Lazarus (of Luke 16) was a parable, promoting Soul sleep.

· Taking Jesus literally in John 6:53, aka the Catholic Eucharist.

Exo 31:3 And I have filled him with the spirit of God, in wisdom, and in understanding, and in knowledge, and in all manner of workmanship,

Deu 1:13 Take you wise men, and understanding, and known among your tribes, and I will make them rulers over you.

Deu 4:6 Keep therefore and do *them;* for this *is* your wisdom and your understanding in the sight of the nations, which shall hear all these statutes, and say, Surely this great nation *is* a wise and understanding people.

1Sa 25:3 Now the name of the man *was* Nabal; and the name of his wife Abigail: and *she was* a woman of good understanding, and of a beautiful countenance: but the man *was* churlish and evil in his doings; and he *was* of the house of Caleb.

1Ki 3:9 Give therefore thy servant an understanding heart to judge thy people, that I may discern between good and bad: for who is able to judge this thy so great a people?

1Ki 7:14 He *was* a widow's son of the tribe of Naphtali, and his father *was* a man of Tyre, a worker in brass: and he was filled with wisdom, and understanding, and cunning to work all works in brass. And he came to king Solomon, and wrought all his work.

1Ch 12:32 And of the children of Issachar, *which were men* that had understanding of the times, to know what Israel ought to do; the heads of them *were* two hundred; and all their brethren *were* at their commandment.

2Ch 26:5 And he sought God in the days of Zechariah, who had understanding in the visions of God: and as long as he sought the LORD, God made him to prosper.

Job 12:3 But I have understanding as well as you; I *am* not inferior to you: yea, who knoweth not such things as these?

Job 12:12 With the ancient *is* wisdom; and in length of days understanding.

Job 17:4 For thou hast hid their heart from understanding: therefore shalt thou not exalt *them.*

Job 28:28 And unto man he said, Behold, the fear of the Lord, that *is* wisdom; and to depart from evil *is* understanding.

Psa 32:9 Be ye not as the horse, *or* as the mule, *which* have no understanding: whose mouth must be held in with bit and bridle, lest they come near unto thee.

Psa 47:7 For God *is* the King of all the earth: sing ye praises with understanding.

Psa 111:10 The fear of the LORD *is* the beginning of wisdom: a good understanding have all they that do *his commandments:* his praise endureth for ever.

Psa_119:34 Give me understanding, and I shall keep thy law; yea, I shall observe it with *my* whole heart.

Psa 119:99 I have more understanding than all my teachers: for thy testimonies *are* my meditation.

Psa 119:104 Through thy precepts I get understanding: therefore I hate every false way.

Psa 147:5 Great *is* our Lord, and of great power: his understanding *is* infinite.

Pro 3:5 Trust in the LORD with all thine heart; and lean not unto thine own understanding.

Pro 3:13 Happy *is* the man *that* findeth wisdom, and the man *that* getteth understanding.

Pro 3:19 The LORD by wisdom hath founded the earth; by understanding hath he established the heavens.

Pro 6:32 *But* whoso committeth adultery with a woman lacketh understanding: he *that* doeth it destroyeth his own soul.

Pro 7:4 Say unto wisdom, Thou *art* my sister; and call understanding *thy* kinswoman:

Pro 9:6 Forsake the foolish, and live; and go in the way of understanding.

Pro 10:13 In the lips of him that hath understanding wisdom is found: but a rod *is* for the back of him that is void of understanding.

Pro 13:15 Good understanding giveth favour: but the way of transgressors *is* hard.

Pro 14:29 *He that is* slow to wrath *is* of great understanding: but *he that is* hasty of spirit exalteth folly.

Pro 16:22 Understanding *is* a wellspring of life unto him that hath it: but the instruction of fools *is* folly.

Pro 18:2 A fool hath no delight in understanding, but that his heart may discover itself.

Pro 19:25 Smite a scorner, and the simple will beware: and reprove one that hath understanding, *and* he will understand knowledge.

Isa 27:11 When the boughs thereof are withered, they shall be broken off: the women come, *and* set them on fire: for it *is* a people of no understanding: therefore he that made them will not have mercy on them, and he that formed them will shew them no favour.

Isa 40:28 Hast thou not known? hast thou not heard, *that* the everlasting God, the LORD, the Creator of the ends of the earth, fainteth not, neither is weary? *there is* no searching of his understanding.

Jer 4:22 For my people *is* foolish, they have not known me; they *are* sottish children, and they have none understanding: they *are* wise to do evil, but to do good they have no knowledge.

Mar 12:33 And to love him with all the heart, and with all the understanding, and with all the soul, and with all the strength, and to love *his* neighbour as himself, is more than all whole burnt offerings and sacrifices.

Luk 24:45 Then opened he their understanding, that they might understand the scriptures,

Rom 1:31 Without understanding, covenantbreakers, without natural affection, implacable, unmerciful:

1Co 1:19 For it is written, I will destroy the wisdom of the wise, and will bring to nothing the understanding of the prudent.

1Co 14:15 What is it then? I will pray with the spirit, and I will pray with the understanding also: I will sing with the spirit, and I will sing with the understanding also.

1Co 14:19 Yet in the church I had rather speak five words with my understanding, that *by my voice* I might teach others also, than ten thousand words in an

unknown tongue.

1Co 14:20 Brethren, be not children in understanding: howbeit in malice be ye children, but in understanding be men.

Php 4:7 And the peace of God, which passeth all understanding, shall keep your hearts and minds through Christ Jesus.

Col 1:9 For this cause we also, since the day we heard *it,* do not cease to pray for you, and to desire that ye might be filled with the knowledge of his will in all wisdom and spiritual understanding;

1Jn 5:20 And we know that the Son of God is come, and hath given us an understanding, that we may know him that is true, and we are in him that is true, *even* in his Son Jesus Christ. This is the true God, and eternal life.

Doctrine

DOCTRINE IS IMPORTANT, doctrine is *very* important! What a man believes and teaches will have an impact on whether he makes New Jerusalem his abode, or hell. If he is an influential teacher, it is even more important that he is able to discern true doctrine from false; as he may be persuading his audience to believe lies. There are countless false doctrines and teachings in the world, this is why we must study the scriptures and lean on the Holy Spirit for guidance and not your own understanding. Believe the scriptures and compare them with other relevant passages as they may shed some light on the harder verses.

Perhaps now would be a good time to bring up Hermeneutics which is "... The science of interpretation and explanation; exegesis; esp., that branch of theology which defines the laws whereby the meaning of the Scriptures is to be ascertained...". *-Websters revised unabridged dictionary 1913.* Surely how one interprets the scriptures affects their doctrine and beliefs.

Undoubtedly much division in the body of Christ has occurred over differing opinions on Church doctrines. It would be ideal if we could all be of the same mind and judgment (1 Cor 1:10), however people can be stubborn and refuse reproof therefore we are told to reject heretics after the first and second admonition (Titus 1:10). The bible is a spiritual book and must be spiritually discerned (John 66:3, 1 Cor 2:14), therefore it's no wonder why there is such a differing opinion on bible teaching; this is most likely because there are so many false converts in the church, although we should also consider that there are many who are babes in Christ who still have much to learn about bible truth (1 Pet 2:2).

The world Christian Encyclopedia (2019) says that their are 45,000 Christian denominations in the world. Is this figure correct? Not really. They are counting the same denomination as a different denomination based on whether it's located in a different country. Example: A USA First Baptist, a Mexican first Baptist, and a Japanese First Baptists would be 3 denominations.

PRO 4:2 FOR I GIVE you good doctrine, forsake ye not my law.

Isa 28:9 Whom shall he teach knowledge? and whom shall he make to understand doctrine? *them that are* weaned from the milk, *and* drawn from the breasts.

Mat 16:12 Then understood they how that he bade *them* not beware of the leaven of bread, but of the doctrine of the Pharisees and of the Sadducees.

Joh 7:17 If any man will do his will, he shall know of the doctrine, whether it be of God, or *whether* I speak of myself.

Act 2:42 And they continued stedfastly in the apostles' doctrine and fellowship, and in breaking of bread, and in prayers.

Rom 6:17 But God be thanked, that ye were the servants of sin, but ye have obeyed from the heart that form of doctrine which was delivered you.

Rom 16:17 Now I beseech you, brethren, mark them which cause divisions and offences contrary to the doctrine which ye have learned; and avoid them.

Eph 4:14 That we *henceforth* be no more children, tossed to and fro, and carried about with every wind of doctrine, by the sleight of men, *and* cunning craftiness, whereby they lie in wait to deceive;

1Ti 1:3 As I besought thee to abide still at Ephesus, when I went into Macedonia, that thou mightest charge some that they teach no other doctrine,

1Ti 4:13 Till I come, give attendance to reading, to exhortation, to doctrine.

1Ti 4:16 Take heed unto thyself, and unto the doctrine; continue in them: for in doing this thou shalt both save thyself, and them that hear thee.

1Ti 6:1 Let as many servants as are under the yoke count their own masters worthy of all honour, that the name of God and *his* doctrine be not blasphemed.

1Ti 6:3 If any man teach otherwise, and consent not to wholesome words, *even* the words of our Lord Jesus Christ, and to the doctrine which is according to godliness;

2Jn 1:9 Whosoever transgresseth, and abideth not in the doctrine of Christ, hath not God. He that abideth in the doctrine of Christ, he hath both the Father and the Son.

Rev 2:14 But I have a few things against thee, because thou hast there them that hold the doctrine of Balaam, who taught Balac to cast a stumblingblock before the children of Israel, to eat things sacrificed unto idols, and to commit fornication.

Rev 2:15 So hast thou also them that hold the doctrine of the Nicolaitans, which thing I hate.

Should we Judge?

ONE OF THE MOST COMMON arguments street preachers hear from skeptics and unbelievers is that we are not supposed to judge. But is this true? Sadly, the verse "Judge not..." has been taken outta context so many times that if I had a dollar for every time this argument was used throughout history, I'd probably be a millionaire; and that is a conservative estimate. One must read the first five verses in Matthew 7 to get the fuller context, which is a condemnation of judging hypocritically (See also Romans 2). The truth is there are verses on promoting judging and condemning the act; therefore it is the way or type of judgment we are doing that is the determining factor on whether or not it is immoral.

As Christians we are to judge actions, both of ourselves and others to see if they are in line with the word of God. If the actions, words, or even our thoughts go against the bible; we are to repent of the said sin, denounce it, and ask forgiveness for it. If we see others doing it we lovingly warn them of the consequences of their actions. Thou shalt not judge is a self-defeating argument. If someone comes to you and says not to judge, they are automatically a hypocrite because they just judged that judging is wrong. We Christians are called to hate the sin, not the sinner. Although we do not know who ultimately will make it to heaven, we can warn people who are in open defiance of the word that their course will lead to destruction.

Everyone makes multiple judgments everyday. What cloths should I wear, what to eat, where I need to go, what to watch, do I stop at that stop sign, do I help that person, etc. So it is easy to see that "thou shalt not judge" is not what the bible teaches. The bible actually says that it is joy to the just to do judgment. From reading Romans 14 and James 4 it would seem that one's attitude and motivation is a key factor on whether judging others is wrong, we see this from the context. It is judging within the context of setting someone at naught or speaking evil against thy brother that is condemned. Scripture actually tells us to judge ourselves and also to judge those in the church, see below.

One way we definitely are not supposed to judge is by appearance (John 7:24), we don't judge people based on the color of their skin, whether or not they have tattoos, or whether or not they look rich (James 2:1-9). We look at the content of their character.

Deu 16:19 Thou shalt not wrest judgment; thou shalt not respect persons, neither take a gift: for a gift doth blind the eyes of the wise, and pervert the words of the righteous.

Deu 17:8 If there arise a matter too hard for thee in judgment, between blood and blood, between plea and plea, and between stroke and stroke, *being* matters of controversy within thy gates: then shalt thou arise, and get thee up into the place which the LORD thy God shall choose;

Deu 17:9 And thou shalt come unto the priests the Levites, and unto the judge that shall be in those days, and enquire; and they shall shew thee the sentence of judgment:

Deu 25:1 If there be a controversy between men, and they come unto judgment, that *the judges* may judge them; then they shall justify the righteous, and condemn the wicked.

Psa 37:28 For the LORD loveth judgment, and forsaketh not his saints; they are preserved for ever: but the seed of the wicked shall be cut off.

Psa 106:3 Blessed *are* they that keep judgment, *and* he that doeth righteousness at all times.

Pro 8:20 I lead in the way of righteousness, in the midst of the paths of judgment:

Pro 21:3 To do justice and judgment *is* more acceptable to the LORD than sacrifice.

Pro 21:7 The robbery of the wicked shall destroy them; because they refuse to do judgment.

Pro 21:15 *It is* joy to the just to do judgment: but destruction *shall be* to the workers of iniquity.

Isa 1:21 How is the faithful city become an harlot! it was full of judgment; righteousness lodged in it; but now murderers.

Isa 5:7 For the vineyard of the LORD of hosts *is* the house of Israel, and the men of Judah his pleasant plant: and he looked for judgment, but behold oppression; for righteousness, but behold a cry.

Isa 56:1 Thus saith the LORD, Keep ye judgment, and do justice: for my salvation *is* near to come, and my righteousness to be revealed.

Isa 61:8 For I the LORD love judgment, I hate robbery for burnt offering; and I will direct their work in truth, and I will make an everlasting covenant with them.

Amo 5:15 Hate the evil, and love the good, and establish judgment in the gate: it may be that the LORD God of hosts will be gracious unto the remnant of Joseph.

Amo 5:24 But let judgment run down as waters, and righteousness as a mighty stream.

Mat 7:1 Judge not, that ye be not judged.

Mat 7:2 For with what judgment ye judge, ye shall be judged: and with what measure ye mete, it shall be measured to you again.

Mat 7:3 And why beholdest thou the mote that is in thy brother's eye, but considerest not the beam that is in thine own eye?

Mat 7:4 Or how wilt thou say to thy brother, Let me pull out the mote out of thine eye; and, behold, a beam *is* in thine own eye?

Mat 7:5 Thou hypocrite, first cast out the beam out of thine own eye; and then shalt thou see clearly to cast out the mote out of thy brother's eye.

Joh 5:22 For the Father judgeth no man, but hath committed all judgment unto the Son:

Joh 7:24 Judge not according to the appearance, but judge righteous judgment.

Rom 2:1 Therefore thou art inexcusable, O man, whosoever thou art that judgest: for wherein thou judgest another, thou condemnest thyself; for thou that judgest doest the same things.

Rom 2:2 But we are sure that the judgment of God is according to truth against them which commit such things.

Rom 2:3 And thinkest thou this, O man, that judgest them which do such things, and doest the same, that thou shalt escape the judgment of God?

Rom 14:4 Who art thou that judgest another man's servant? to his own master he standeth or falleth. Yea, he shall be holden up: for God is able to make him stand.

Rom 14:10 But why dost thou judge thy brother? or why dost thou set at nought thy brother? for we shall all stand before the judgment seat of Christ.

Rom 14:13 Let us not therefore judge one another any more: but judge this rather, that no man put a stumblingblock or an occasion to fall in *his* brother's way.

1Co 2:15 But he that is spiritual judgeth all things, yet he himself is judged of no man.

1Co 4:3 But with me it is a very small thing that I should be judged of you, or of man's judgment: yea, I judge not mine own self.

1Co 4:5 Therefore judge nothing before the time, until the Lord come, who both will bring to light the hidden things of darkness, and will make manifest the counsels of the hearts: and then shall every man have praise of God.

1Co 5:12 For what have I to do to judge them also that are without? do not ye judge them that are within?

1Co 6:2 Do ye not know that the saints shall judge the world? and if the world shall be judged by you, are ye unworthy to judge the smallest matters?

1Co 6:3 Know ye not that we shall judge angels? how much more things that pertain to this life?

1Co 6:4 If then ye have judgments of things pertaining to this life, set them to judge who are least esteemed in the church.

1Co 6:5 I speak to your shame. Is it so, that there is not a wise man among you? no, not one that shall be able to judge between his brethren?

1Co 10:15 I speak as to wise men; judge ye what I say.

1Co 11:31 For if we would judge ourselves, we should not be judged.

1Co 14:29 Let the prophets speak two or three, and let the other judge.

2Co 10:12 For we dare not make ourselves of the number, or compare ourselves with some that commend themselves: but they measuring themselves by themselves, and comparing themselves among themselves, are not wise.

2Ti 4:1 I charge *thee* therefore before God, and the Lord Jesus Christ, who shall judge the quick and the dead at his appearing and his kingdom;

Heb 12:23 To the general assembly and church of the firstborn, which are written in heaven, and to God the Judge of all, and to the spirits of just men made perfect,

Jas 4:11 Speak not evil one of another, brethren. He that speaketh evil of *his* brother, and judgeth his brother, speaketh evil of the law, and judgeth the law: but if thou judge the law, thou art not a doer of the law, but a judge.

Rev 20:12 And I saw the dead, small and great, stand before God; and the books were opened: and another book was opened, which is *the book* of life: and the dead were judged out of those things which were written in the books, according to their works.

Rebuke, Reproof, Correction, etc.

CORRECTION CAN BE A hard thing to handle. Sometimes it isn't easy to admit when you are wrong, but something we must realize is that correction, reproof and even rebuke are not sinful but rather loving. Parents warn their children not to play in the street because they understand the danger that can accompany it. Likewise when a fellow Christian warns another believer of a particular sin they are committing, it isn't hateful but loving. And when street preaching warn the ungodly of the judgment to come; they are not being mean, they are speaking out of concern for their spiritual well-being.

Things like drugs, too much junk food, abuse, promiscuity, gambling, as well as what you watch and listen to can have a negative impact on one's physical, mental, financial, and spiritual health; therefore we should not resent those that would warn us of the consequences of said actions. We must guard against pride and humble ourselves before our creator. If we don't accept criticism well, this means that we think we are good enough and that we don't need to become more like Christ; that we are already his equal. May this never be! We all have areas of improvement and as professing believers in Christ we should always be trying to become more like the Saviour.

Is there anyone that we are not to reprove or rebuke? Well the scripture are clear that we are not to reprove scorners Proverbs 9:7, instead we are are to cast them out (Prov 22:10). We also are not to rebuke elders but rather entreat them as fathers, this would seem to be a more gentle approach to correction. We do not rebuke in our own authority but in Jesus authority, for it is Jesus' word that carries the authority.

LEV 19:17 THOU SHALT not hate thy brother in thine heart: thou shalt in any wise rebuke thy neighbour, and not suffer sin upon him.

Deu 28:20 The LORD shall send upon thee cursing, vexation, and rebuke, in all that thou settest thine hand unto for to do, until thou be destroyed, and until thou perish quickly; because of the wickedness of thy doings, whereby thou hast forsaken me.

Psa 141:5 Let the righteous smite me; *it shall be* a kindness: and let him reprove me; *it shall be* an excellent oil, *which* shall not break my head: for yet my prayer also *shall be* in their calamities.

Pro 9:8 Reprove not a scorner, lest he hate thee: rebuke a wise man, and he will love thee.

Pro 10:17 He *is in* the way of life that keepeth instruction: but he that refuseth reproof erreth.

Pro 12:1 Whoso loveth instruction loveth knowledge: but he that hateth reproof *is* brutish.

Pro 13:18 Poverty and shame *shall be to* him that refuseth instruction: but he that regardeth reproof shall be honoured.

Pro 15:5 A fool despiseth his father's instruction: but he that regardeth reproof is prudent.

Pro 15:10 Correction *is* grievous unto him that forsaketh the way: *and* he that hateth reproof shall die.

Pro 15:31 The ear that heareth the reproof of life abideth among the wise.

Pro 15:32 He that refuseth instruction despiseth his own soul: but he that heareth reproof getteth understanding.

Pro 17:10 A reproof entereth more into a wise man than an hundred stripes into a fool.

Pro 19:25 Smite a scorner, and the simple will beware: and reprove one that hath understanding, *and* he will understand knowledge.

Pro 27:5 Open rebuke *is* better than secret love.

Pro 27:6 Faithful *are* the wounds of a friend; but the kisses of an enemy *are* deceitful.

Ecc 4:13 Better *is* a poor and a wise child than an old and foolish king, who will no more be admonished.

Ecc 7:5 *It is* better to hear the rebuke of the wise, than for a man to hear the song of fools.

Luk 17:3 Take heed to yourselves: If thy brother trespass against thee, rebuke him; and if he repent, forgive him.

Eph 5:11 And have no fellowship with the unfruitful works of darkness, but rather reprove *them.*

Php 2:15 That ye may be blameless and harmless, the sons of God, without rebuke, in the midst of a crooked and perverse nation, among whom ye shine as lights in the world;

1Ti 5:1 Rebuke not an elder, but intreat *him* as a father; *and* the younger men as brethren;

1Ti 5:20 Them that sin rebuke before all, that others also may fear.

2Ti 3:16 All scripture *is* given by inspiration of God, and *is* profitable for doctrine, for reproof, for correction, for instruction in righteousness:

2Ti 4:2 Preach the word; be instant in season, out of season; reprove, rebuke, exhort with all longsuffering and doctrine.

Tit 1:13 This witness is true. Wherefore rebuke them sharply, that they may be sound in the faith;

Tit 2:15 These things speak, and exhort, and rebuke with all authority. Let no man despise thee.

Jud 1:9 Yet Michael the archangel, when contending with the devil he disputed about the body of Moses, durst not bring against him a railing accusation, but said, The Lord rebuke thee.

Rev 3:19 As many as I love, I rebuke and chasten: be zealous therefore, and repent.

Colors

THIS STUDY WILL BE about the Colors of the Rainbow. What does each of the Colors signify or correlate to in the scriptures. Nowadays people associate the rainbow with gay pride. The rainbow flag is a common accessory among pride parades. While the gay pride flag contains six colors of the rainbow, the actual rainbow (which is a token of the Lord's Covenant with the earth not to flood the earth again), contains seven colors.

This study contains the three primary colors (which bring to remembrance the three members of the Godhead), three secondary colors; which are combinations of the three primary colors, and a seventh color which is a combination of a primary and a secondary color.

Red- God the Son's Blood, Cleanses from Sin, Righteousness, Forgiveness, Redemption

2Ki 3:22 And they rose up early in the morning, and the sun shone upon the water, and the Moabites saw the water on the other side *as* red as blood:

1Jn 1:7 But if we walk in the light, as he is in the light, we have fellowship one with another, and the blood of Jesus Christ his Son cleanseth us from all sin.

Blue- God the Father's Law, His Character, and Throne

Num 15:38 Speak unto the children of Israel, and bid them that they make them fringes in the borders of their garments throughout their generations, and that they put upon the fringe of the borders a ribband of blue:

Num 15:39 And it shall be unto you for a fringe, that ye may look upon it, and remember all the commandments of the LORD, and do them; and that ye seek not after your own heart and your own eyes, after which ye use to go a whoring:

Exo 24:10 And they saw the God of Israel: and *there was* under his feet as it were a paved work of a sapphire stone, and as it were the body of heaven in *his* clearness.

Yellow- Reminds us of the Spirit (Love, Hope, Comfort, Truth)

Psa 68:13 Though ye have lien among the pots, *yet shall ye be as* the wings of a dove covered with silver, and her feathers with yellow gold.

Joh 16:13 Howbeit when he, the Spirit of truth, is come, he will guide you into all truth: for he shall not speak of himself; but whatsoever he shall hear, *that* shall he speak: and he will shew you things to come.

Rom 5:5 And hope maketh not ashamed; because the love of God is shed abroad in our hearts by the Holy Ghost which is given unto us.

Green- Trust, Mercy, Hope

Psa 52:8 But I *am* like a green olive tree in the house of God: I trust in the mercy of God for ever and ever.

Jer 17:7 Blessed *is* the man that trusteth in the LORD, and whose hope the LORD is.

Purple- Royalty, Our Inheritance, Protection

Luk 16:19 There was a certain rich man, which was clothed in purple and fine linen, and fared sumptuously every day:

Joh 19:2 And the soldiers platted a crown of thorns, and put *it* on his head, and they put on him a purple robe,

1Pe 2:9 But ye *are* a chosen generation, a royal priesthood, an holy nation, a peculiar people; that ye should shew forth the praises of him who hath called you out of darkness into his marvellous light:

Orange (Amber)- Fire, Light, Power, Faith, Praise, Glory, Honour,

Eze 1:27 And I saw as the colour of amber, as the appearance of fire round about within it, from the appearance of his loins even upward, and from the appearance of his loins even downward, I saw as it were the appearance of fire, and it had brightness round about.

Mat 3:11 I indeed baptize you with water unto repentance: but he that cometh after me is mightier than I, whose shoes I am not worthy to bear: he shall baptize you with the Holy Ghost, and *with* fire:

1Pe 1:7 That the trial of your faith, being much more precious than of gold that perisheth, though it be tried with fire, might be found unto praise and honour and glory at the appearing of Jesus Christ:

Indigo (Purple + Blue)- Old Testament Tabernacle, Sanctification?

Exo 28:15 And thou shalt make the breastplate of judgment with cunning work; after the work of the ephod thou shalt make it; *of* gold, *of* blue, and *of* purple, and *of* scarlet, and *of* fine twined linen, shalt thou make it.

Exo 36:8 And every wise hearted man among them that wrought the work of the tabernacle made ten curtains *of* fine twined linen, and blue, and purple, and scarlet: *with* cherubims of cunning work made he them.

Exo 39:1 And of the blue, and purple, and scarlet, they made cloths of service, to do service in the holy *place,* and made the holy garments for Aaron; as the LORD commanded Moses.

Please note the reason I put a question mark next to the sanctification is simply because the word indigo isn't in scripture and of how I obtained this information. I got it from a Youtube video titled "Ex-Gay Reveals the Real Meaning of the Rainbow | Mind-blown!! | LED Live". Right around the 59:30 to just after the 1 hr mark, the speaker informs us the Lord told him as he was waking up if there was anywhere in the bible blue and purple are mentioned at the same time? (not a quote).

It's not that I don't think the Lord speaks to us today, because I most certainly do, and I really don't know enough about the speaker in the video to make any negative judgment about him saving he mentions the "spirit of prophecy" which automatically should put up some red flags to anyone familiar with 7th day advent-ism. This is a book that was written by Ellen G. White, and should be avoided at all costs. This isn't the place for me to go into all the details of the false teachings of 7th day advent-ism; so I will just have to let my readers look that up on their own. I apologize for the side tangent, let's get back on topic.

———

BONUS COLOR: This isn't a color of the rainbow, but rather a mixture of the first six colors of the color wheel. So the following color is kind of a way of showing the Lord has all these wonderful attributes intended for us.

Brown- Mankind? (also stated by same person in video)

Gen 2:7 And the LORD God formed man *of* the dust of the ground, and breathed into his nostrils the breath of life; and man became a living soul.

Gen 3:19 In the sweat of thy face shalt thou eat bread, till thou return unto the ground; for out of it wast thou taken: for dust thou *art,* and unto dust shalt thou return.

Salvation

THIS STUDY IS COMPRISED a little differently than most in this book. Instead of going completely chronologically (or how they are listed in scripture), I took the liberty to arrange these verses concerning salvation by categories. So what are the most important things to realize about salvation? First we must realize how to be saved, which is actually quite simple. To be saved one must... Admit your a sinner, Believe Jesus paid for your sins on the cross, and repent of your sins. That's pretty much it. Also if someone is saved we should expect them to exhibit the fruits of the Spirit, if they truly are born again.

There are two important things we should remember concerning Salvation. The first of the two is that it is a gift of God, you can't earn it by doing good works (good works cannot erase a sin debt; only Jesus' blood can do that), and number two although nobody can pluck you from the Father's hand, and you can rest assured that God has saved you, this doesn't mean you can't backslide and forfeit your salvation through willful habitual sin. In other words once saved always saved is a lie.

---

1. THE GOSPEL.

1Co 15:1 Moreover, brethren, I declare unto you the gospel which I preached unto you, which also ye have received, and wherein ye stand;

1Co 15:2 By which also ye are saved, if ye keep in memory what I preached unto you, unless ye have believed in vain.

1Co 15:3 For I delivered unto you first of all that which I also received, how that Christ died for our sins according to the scriptures;

1Co 15:4 And that he was buried, and that he rose again the third day according to the scriptures:

1Co 15:5 And that he was seen of Cephas, then of the twelve:

1Co 15:6 After that, he was seen of above five hundred brethren at once; of whom the greater part remain unto this present, but some are fallen asleep.

1Co 15:7 After that, he was seen of James; then of all the apostles.

1Co 15:8 And last of all he was seen of me also, as of one born out of due time.

---

2. ACQUIRED THROUGH faith not works.

Rom 4:2 For if Abraham were justified by works, he hath *whereof* to glory; but not before God.

Rom 4:3 For what saith the scripture? Abraham believed God, and it was counted unto him for righteousness.

Rom 4:4 Now to him that worketh is the reward not reckoned of grace, but of debt.

Rom 4:5 But to him that worketh not, but believeth on him that justifieth the ungodly, his faith is counted for righteousness.

Rom 4:6 Even as David also describeth the blessedness of the man, unto whom God imputeth righteousness without works,

Rom 11:6 And if by grace, then *is it* no more of works: otherwise grace is no more grace. But if *it be* of works, then is it no more grace: otherwise work is no more work.

Gal 3:11 But that no man is justified by the law in the sight of God, *it is* evident: for, The just shall live by faith.

Eph 2:8 For by grace are ye saved through faith; and that not of yourselves: *it is* the gift of God:

Eph 2:9 Not of works, lest any man should boast.

Tit 3:5 Not by works of righteousness which we have done, but according to his mercy he saved us, by the washing of regeneration, and renewing of the Holy Ghost;

---

3. FEW OBTAIN IT.

Mat 7:13 Enter ye in at the strait gate: for wide *is* the gate, and broad *is* the way, that leadeth to destruction, and many there be which go in thereat:

Mat 7:14 Because strait *is* the gate, and narrow *is* the way, which leadeth unto life, and few there be that find it.

Mat 7:21 Not every one that saith unto me, Lord, Lord, shall enter into the kingdom of heaven; but he that doeth the will of my Father which is in heaven.

Mar 4:14 The sower soweth the word.

Mar 4:15 And these are they by the way side, where the word is sown; but when they have heard, Satan cometh immediately, and taketh away the word that was sown in their hearts.

Mar 4:16 And these are they likewise which are sown on stony ground; who, when they have heard the word, immediately receive it with gladness;

Mar 4:17 And have no root in themselves, and so endure but for a time: afterward, when affliction or persecution ariseth for the word's sake, immediately they are offended.

Mar 4:18 And these are they which are sown among thorns; such as hear the word,

Mar 4:19 And the cares of this world, and the deceitfulness of riches, and the lusts of other things entering in, choke the word, and it becometh unfruitful.

Mar 4:20 And these are they which are sown on good ground; such as hear the word, and receive *it,* and bring forth fruit, some thirtyfold, some sixty, and some an hundred.

Luk 13:23 Then said one unto him, Lord, are there few that be saved? And he said unto them,

Luk 13:24 Strive to enter in at the strait gate: for many, I say unto you, will seek to enter in, and shall not be able.

Luk 13:25 When once the master of the house is risen up, and hath shut to the door, and ye begin to stand without, and to knock at the door, saying, Lord, Lord, open unto us; and he shall answer and say unto you, I know you not whence ye are:

Joh 14:6 Jesus saith unto him, I am the way, the truth, and the life: no man cometh unto the Father, but by me.

---

4. THE IMPORTANCE OF repentance and having good fruit/works. (Works prove living faith).

Mat 7:18 A good tree cannot bring forth evil fruit, neither *can* a corrupt tree bring forth good fruit.

Mar 1:4 John did baptize in the wilderness, and preach the baptism of repentance for the remission of sins.

Luk 5:32 I came not to call the righteous, but sinners to repentance.

Luk 24:47 And that repentance and remission of sins should be preached in his name among all nations, beginning at Jerusalem.

Joh 15:2 Every branch in me that beareth not fruit he taketh away: and every *branch* that beareth fruit, he purgeth it, that it may bring forth more fruit.

Act 11:18 When they heard these things, they held their peace, and glorified God, saying, Then hath God also to the Gentiles granted repentance unto life.

Act 20:21 Testifying both to the Jews, and also to the Greeks, repentance toward God, and faith toward our Lord Jesus Christ.

Act 26:20 But shewed first unto them of Damascus, and at Jerusalem, and throughout all the coasts of Judaea, and *then* to the Gentiles, that they should repent and turn to God, and do works meet for repentance.

2Co 7:10 For godly sorrow worketh repentance to salvation not to be repented of: but the sorrow of the world worketh death.

Eph 2:10 For we are his workmanship, created in Christ Jesus unto good works, which God hath before ordained that we should walk in them.

Jas 2:14 What *doth it* profit, my brethren, though a man say he hath faith, and have not works? can faith save him?

Jas 2:17 Even so faith, if it hath not works, is dead, being alone.

Jas 2:18 Yea, a man may say, Thou hast faith, and I have works: shew me thy faith without thy works, and I will shew thee my faith by my works.

---

5. VERSES WITH THE word salvation.

2Sa 22:3 The God of my rock; in him will I trust: *he is* my shield, and the horn of my salvation, my high tower, and my refuge, my saviour; thou savest me from violence.

Psa 3:8 Salvation *belongeth* unto the LORD: thy blessing *is* upon thy people. Selah.

Psa 27:1 *A Psalm* of David. The LORD *is* my light and my salvation; whom shall I fear? the LORD *is* the strength of my life; of whom shall I be afraid?

Psa 40:10 I have not hid thy righteousness within my heart; I have declared thy faithfulness and thy salvation: I have not concealed thy lovingkindness and thy truth from the great congregation.

Psa 40:16 Let all those that seek thee rejoice and be glad in thee: let such as love thy salvation say continually, The LORD be magnified.

Psa 51:12 Restore unto me the joy of thy salvation; and uphold me *with thy* free spirit.

Psa 68:20 *He that is* our God *is* the God of salvation; and unto GOD the Lord *belong* the issues from death.

Psa 119:155 Salvation *is* far from the wicked: for they seek not thy statutes.

Psa 119:174 I have longed for thy salvation, O LORD; and thy law *is* my delight.

Psa 149:4 For the LORD taketh pleasure in his people: he will beautify the meek with salvation.

Isa 12:2 Behold, God *is* my salvation; I will trust, and not be afraid: for the LORD JEHOVAH *is* my strength and *my* song; he also is become my salvation.

Isa 12:3 Therefore with joy shall ye draw water out of the wells of salvation.

Isa 51:5 My righteousness *is* near; my salvation is gone forth, and mine arms shall judge the people; the isles shall wait upon me, and on mine arm shall they trust.

Isa 59:16 And he saw that *there was* no man, and wondered that *there was* no intercessor: therefore his arm brought salvation unto him; and his righteousness, it sustained him.

Joh 4:22 Ye worship ye know not what: we know what we worship: for salvation is of the Jews.

Rom 1:16 For I am not ashamed of the gospel of Christ: for it is the power of God unto salvation to every one that believeth; to the Jew first, and also to the Greek.

Rom 10:10 For with the heart man believeth unto righteousness; and with the mouth confession is made unto salvation.

Rom 11:11 I say then, Have they stumbled that they should fall? God forbid: but *rather* through their fall salvation *is come* unto the Gentiles, for to provoke them to jealousy.

1Th 5:8 But let us, who are of the day, be sober, putting on the breastplate of faith and love; and for an helmet, the hope of salvation.

Tit 2:11 For the grace of God that bringeth salvation hath appeared to all men,

1Pe 1:9 Receiving the end of your faith, *even* the salvation of *your* souls.

Repentance

WHAT IS REPENTANCE? Repentance is a change of mind that leads to a change in action. A turning from sin to God. Although in God's case it is more like he expressing sorrow over or turning from doing something, not that he sinned. Repentance is a vital part of Salvation, although we cannot be good enough to merit heaven; there still needs to be a contrition over wrongdoing and a resolve to overcome whatever sinful habit it may be that we have committed, or are continuing to commit. We cannot expect to overcome sin on our own, we need Jesus' help, we must rely on his forgiveness, strength, and cleansing in fighting this lifelong battle.

As we grow in our walk with Christ, and in our sanctification, we can also expect to be growing in our repentance as well. Things we didn't know were sin when we were unbelievers or babes in Christ, will eventually be made clear to us later and it is then that we must renounce those things and turn from them. There will be things that you find out in scripture that are sin, and there are things not listed in scripture that your conscience will convict you of; which then you should listen to your conscience even though it's not mentioned in the word.

There is this teaching called "once saved always saved" (OSAS), it basically says that as long as you truly believed at one point in your life, then that's it your saved and nothing you do can make you unsaved. Under this doctrine, it doesn't matter if you are living in habitual or willful sin, backslide, stop praying, etc. Your going to heaven no matter what. Is this true? Or can a person be genuinely saved continue for a season and then fall away from the faith and lose their salvation. Their are many bible verses which refute OSAS but I plan on covering that in my second volume (Lord willing), so I won't go into great detail about that here.

There are some people who profess belief in "faith only" otherwise known as easy believism, they think repentance isn't necessary for salvation. This simply is not true. The book of 2nd chronicles 7 says that God will forgive their sin if they turn from their wicked ways, and if they say "we'll that's the old testament we are not under the law". Well we are not under Israel's civil and ceremonial laws but the moral law still stands. All we have to do is look at Acts 8:22 to see that forgiveness is still conditional based on repentance. 2 Corinthians 7 also tells that godly sorrow worketh repentance to salvation.

So are we saved by faith or works then? Please don't misunderstand me, I do not advocate for works salvation, it is only by the imputed righteousness of Christ that we can be saved. Works do not save, or in other words we cannot bribe God with our good works to let us into heaven. Good works don't erase sin, Jesus' blood does. However there are varying degrees of faith, and as James declares there is even such as thing as dead faith (which cannot save). What is dead faith? Dead faith is faith without works. You see, saying works save is putting the cart before the horse, works are the evidence of saving/living/ genuine/ faith.

———————

2CH 7:14 IF MY PEOPLE, which are called by my name, shall humble themselves, and pray, and seek my face, and turn from their wicked ways; then will I hear from heaven, and will forgive their sin, and will heal their land.

Psa 55:19 God shall hear, and afflict them, even he that abideth of old. Selah. Because they have no changes, therefore they fear not God.

Pro 28:13 He that covereth his sins shall not prosper: but whoso confesseth and forsaketh *them* shall have mercy.

Eze 18:21 But if the wicked will turn from all his sins that he hath committed, and keep all my statutes, and do that which is lawful and right, he shall surely live, he shall not die.

Eze 18:22 All his transgressions that he hath committed, they shall not be mentioned unto him: in his righteousness that he hath done he shall live.

Jon 3:7 And he caused *it* to be proclaimed and published through Nineveh by the decree of the king and his nobles, saying, Let neither man nor beast, herd nor flock, taste any thing: let them not feed, nor drink water:

Jon 3:8 But let man and beast be covered with sackcloth, and cry mightily unto God: yea, let them turn every one from his evil way, and from the violence that *is* in their hands.

Jon 3:9 Who can tell *if* God will turn and repent, and turn away from his fierce anger, that we perish not?

Jon 3:10 And God saw their works, that they turned from their evil way; and God repented of the evil, that he had said that he would do unto them; and he did *it* not.

Mat 12:41 The men of Nineveh shall rise in judgment with this generation, and shall condemn it: because they repented at the preaching of Jonas; and, behold, a greater than Jonas *is* here.

Mat 4:17 From that time Jesus began to preach, and to say, Repent: for the kingdom of heaven is at hand.

Luk 5:32 I came not to call the righteous, but sinners to repentance.

Luk 13:5 I tell you, Nay: but, except ye repent, ye shall all likewise perish.

Joh 5:14 Afterward Jesus findeth him in the temple, and said unto him, Behold, thou art made whole: sin no more, lest a worse thing come unto thee.

Joh 8:11 She said, No man, Lord. And Jesus said unto her, Neither do I condemn thee: go, and sin no more.

Act 8:22 Repent therefore of this thy wickedness, and pray God, if perhaps the thought of thine heart may be forgiven thee.

Act 20:21 Testifying both to the Jews, and also to the Greeks, repentance toward God, and faith toward our Lord Jesus Christ.

2Co 7:8 For though I made you sorry with a letter, I do not repent, though I did repent: for I perceive that the same epistle hath made you sorry, though *it were* but for a season.

2Co 7:9 Now I rejoice, not that ye were made sorry, but that ye sorrowed to repentance: for ye were made sorry after a godly manner, that ye might receive damage by us in nothing.

2Co 7:10 For godly sorrow worketh repentance to salvation not to be repented of: but the sorrow of the world worketh death.

2Co 7:11 For behold this selfsame thing, that ye sorrowed after a godly sort, what carefulness it wrought in you, yea, *what* clearing of yourselves, yea, *what* indignation, yea, *what* fear, yea, *what* vehement desire, yea, *what* zeal, yea, *what* revenge! In all *things* ye have approved yourselves to be clear in this matter.

2Co 12:21 *And* lest, when I come again, my God will humble me among you, and *that* I shall bewail many which have sinned already, and have not repented of the uncleanness and fornication and lasciviousness which they have committed.

2Ti 2:19 Nevertheless the foundation of God standeth sure, having this seal, The Lord knoweth them that are his. And, Let every one that nameth the name of Christ depart from iniquity.

Tit 2:12 Teaching us that, denying ungodliness and worldly lusts, we should live soberly, righteously, and godly, in this present world;

Jas 1:22 But be ye doers of the word, and not hearers only, deceiving your own selves.

2Pe 3:9 The Lord is not slack concerning his promise, as some men count slackness; but is longsuffering to us-ward, not willing that any should perish, but that all should come to repentance.

Rev 2:5 Remember therefore from whence thou art fallen, and repent, and do the first works; or else I will come unto thee quickly, and will remove thy candlestick out of his place, except thou repent.

Rev 2:22 Behold, I will cast her into a bed, and them that commit adultery with her into great tribulation, except they repent of their deeds.

Gospel In Genesis Genealogy

WHAT FOLLOWS IS AN astounding piece of valuable information. If you look up the meaning of the names of the first 9 people in the genealogy of Genesis 5, we see a prophecy of Jesus death for the sin of the world.

Hebrew - English

Adam - Man

Seth - Appointed

Enosh - Mortal

Kenan - Sorrow;

Mahalalel - The Blessed God

Jared - Shall come down

Enoch - Teaching

Methuselah - His death shall bring

Lamech - The Despairing

Noah - Rest, or comfort.

New Birth

THE NEW BIRTH OR BEING born again is the event when someone who wasn't saved at first, after believing the gospel and repenting of their sins, receives the Holy Spirit and is changed into a new creature, and is now a child of God. Like salvation, you cannot earn this, it is the gift of God. Another way to say it is that you are now spiritually alive; and as such your mind starts to change so that you no longer desire the things that are an offense to the thrice holy God; but rather you desire to live a holy, Jesus-honoring life. Once born again, God's Spirit will enable you to overcome when temptation arises.

Eze 36:25 Then will I sprinkle clean water upon you, and ye shall be clean: from all your filthiness, and from all your idols, will I cleanse you.

Eze 36:26 A new heart also will I give you, and a new spirit will I put within you: and I will take away the stony heart out of your flesh, and I will give you an heart of flesh.

Eze 36:27 And I will put my spirit within you, and cause you to walk in my statutes, and ye shall keep my judgments, and do *them*.

Joh 3:3 Jesus answered and said unto him, Verily, verily, I say unto thee, Except a man be born again, he cannot see the kingdom of God.

Joh 3:4 Nicodemus saith unto him, How can a man be born when he is old? can he enter the second time into his mother's womb, and be born?

Joh 3:5 Jesus answered, Verily, verily, I say unto thee, Except a man be born of water and *of* the Spirit, he cannot enter into the kingdom of God.

Joh 3:6 That which is born of the flesh is flesh; and that which is born of the Spirit is spirit.

Joh 3:7 Marvel not that I said unto thee, Ye must be born again.

Joh 3:8 The wind bloweth where it listeth, and thou hearest the sound thereof, but canst not tell whence it cometh, and whither it goeth: so is every one that is born of the Spirit.

Rom 6:3 Know ye not, that so many of us as were baptized into Jesus Christ were baptized into his death?

Rom 6:4 Therefore we are buried with him by baptism into death: that like as Christ was raised up from the dead by the glory of the Father, even so we also should walk in newness of life.

Rom 6:5 For if we have been planted together in the likeness of his death, we shall be also *in the likeness* of *his* resurrection:

Rom 6:10 For in that he died, he died unto sin once: but in that he liveth, he liveth unto God.

Rom 6:11 Likewise reckon ye also yourselves to be dead indeed unto sin, but alive unto God through Jesus Christ our Lord.

2Co 5:17 Therefore if any man *be* in Christ, *he is* a new creature: old things are passed away; behold, all things are become new.

Gal 6:15 For in Christ Jesus neither circumcision availeth any thing, nor uncircumcision, but a new creature.

Eph 4:22 That ye put off concerning the former conversation the old man, which is corrupt according to the deceitful lusts;

Eph 4:23 And be renewed in the spirit of your mind;

Eph 4:24 And that ye put on the new man, which after God is created in righteousness and true holiness.

Col 3:9 Lie not one to another, seeing that ye have put off the old man with his deeds;

Col 3:10 And have put on the new *man,* which is renewed in knowledge after the image of him that created him:

1Pe 1:23 Being born again, not of corruptible seed, but of incorruptible, by the word of God, which liveth and abideth for ever.

Sanctification

FOR THIS STUDY WE WILL be going over the topic of Sanctification which Websters Revised Unabridged Dictionary (1913) defines as: "1. The act of sanctifying or making holy; the state of being sanctified or made holy; esp. (Theol.), the act of God's grace by which the affections of men are purified, or alienated from sin and the world, and exalted to a supreme love to God; also, the state of being thus purified or sanctified..."

Sanctification can also been seen as the lifelong process wherewithal God purges us from our old sinful ways and shapes us more and more to be conformed to that of his dear Perfect Son (Rom 8:29,Gal 4:19). One thing we need to realize is that everyone is on different levels of sanctification. Do not expect someone who just got saved to be at the same level as someone who has been walking with the Lord for thirty years. However age alone doesn't necessarily imply more sanctification, there are many professing believers out there and in the church who have been believers for decades and yet still resemble the world in many aspects. Why is this? Two words. False Converts. They are too preoccupied/enamored with the world to focus on the things above to bear fruit. Jesus calls these type of people, the thorny ground.

Some examples of Sanctification:

- **Listening to Godly Music instead of Secular**

- **Watching Sermons instead of Corrupt TV series**

- **Quitting Smoking, Drugs, Cursing, Unforgivness, etc**

Some of my personal examples of sanctification include: Stopped listening to ungodly music, Exercising judgment if I decide to play video games (avoiding magic, considering violent contents, etc), Stopped watching horror movies, stopped watching P*rn, stopped watching dragonball and other ungodly anime shows such as Inuyasha and Yu Yu hakusho, quit celebration pagan holidays, and i still have much growing to do.

Exo 28:41 And thou shalt put them upon Aaron thy brother, and his sons with him; and shalt anoint them, and consecrate them, and sanctify them, that they may minister unto me in the priest's office.

Lev 11:44 For I *am* the LORD your God: ye shall therefore sanctify yourselves, and ye shall be holy; for I *am* holy: neither shall ye defile yourselves with any manner of creeping thing that creepeth upon the earth.

Lev 20:8 And ye shall keep my statutes, and do them: I *am* the LORD which sanctify you.

Lev 27:14 And when a man shall sanctify his house *to be* holy unto the LORD, then the priest shall estimate it, whether it be good or bad: as the priest shall estimate it, so shall it stand.

Num 8:17 For all the firstborn of the children of Israel *are* mine, *both* man and beast: on the day that I smote every firstborn in the land of Egypt I sanctified them for myself.

Deu 15:19 All the firstling males that come of thy herd and of thy flock thou shalt sanctify unto the LORD thy God: thou shalt do no work with the firstling of thy bullock, nor shear the firstling of thy sheep.

1Ch 23:13 The sons of Amram; Aaron and Moses: and Aaron was separated, that he should sanctify the most holy things, he and his sons for ever, to burn incense before the LORD, to minister unto him, and to bless in his name for ever.

2Ch 29:5 And said unto them, Hear me, ye Levites, sanctify now yourselves, and sanctify the house of the LORD God of your fathers, and carry forth the filthiness out of the holy *place.*

2Ch 30:3 For they could not keep it at that time, because the priests had not sanctified themselves sufficiently, neither had the people gathered themselves together to Jerusalem.

Neh 12:47 And all Israel in the days of Zerubbabel, and in the days of Nehemiah, gave the portions of the singers and the porters, every day his portion: and they sanctified *holy things* unto the Levites; and the Levites sanctified *them* unto the children of Aaron.

Isa 8:13 Sanctify the LORD of hosts himself; and *let* him *be* your fear, and *let* him *be* your dread.

Eze 37:28 And the heathen shall know that I the LORD do sanctify Israel, when my sanctuary shall be in the midst of them for evermore.

Joh 17:17 Sanctify them through thy truth: thy word is truth.

Act 26:18 To open their eyes, *and* to turn *them* from darkness to light, and *from* the power of Satan unto God, that they may receive forgiveness of sins, and inheritance among them which are sanctified by faith that is in me.

Rom 12:2 And be not conformed to this world: but be ye transformed by the renewing of your mind, that ye may prove what *is* that good, and acceptable, and perfect, will of God.

Rom 15:16 That I should be the minister of Jesus Christ to the Gentiles, ministering the gospel of God, that the offering up of the Gentiles might be acceptable, being sanctified by the Holy Ghost.

1Co 7:14 For the unbelieving husband is sanctified by the wife, and the unbelieving wife is

sanctified by the husband: else were your children unclean; but now are they holy.

2Co 6:14 Be ye not unequally yoked together with unbelievers: for what fellowship hath righteousness with unrighteousness? and what communion hath light with darkness?

Eph 5:26 That he might sanctify and cleanse it with the washing of water by the word,

2Th 2:13 But we are bound to give thanks alway to God for you, brethren beloved of the Lord, because God hath from the beginning chosen you to salvation through sanctification of the Spirit and belief of the truth:

1Ti 4:5 For it is sanctified by the word of God and prayer.

2Ti 2:21 If a man therefore purge himself from these, he shall be a vessel unto honour, sanctified, and meet for the master's use, *and* prepared unto every good work.

Heb 2:11 For both he that sanctifieth and they who are sanctified *are* all of one: for which cause he is not ashamed to call them brethren,

Heb 13:12 Wherefore Jesus also, that he might sanctify the people with his own blood, suffered without the gate.

Jas 4:4 Ye adulterers and adulteresses, know ye not that the friendship of the world is enmity with God? whosoever therefore will be a friend of the world is the enemy of God.

1Pe 1:2 Elect according to the foreknowledge of God the Father, through sanctification of the Spirit, unto obedience and sprinkling of the blood of Jesus Christ: Grace unto you, and peace, be multiplied.

1Pe 2:9 But ye *are* a chosen generation, a royal priesthood, an holy nation, a peculiar people; that ye should shew forth the praises of him who hath called you out of darkness into his marvellous light:

Jud 1:1 Jude, the servant of Jesus Christ, and brother of James, to them that are sanctified by God the Father, and preserved in Jesus Christ, *and* called:

Preaching

SO WHAT IS PREACHING? Or Rather what should Christian's preach? From the verses that I will list below we see that we are to preach repentance and remission (forgiveness) of sins, the gospel (Jesus' death, burial, and resurrection), and well that's the main thing.

Preaching is a command in scripture, the gospel should be preached to everyone, from Mat 10:27 I gather that we should be loud when we preach so that those passing by may hear, I think It's good to memorize relevant bible verses to quote aloud; after all faith coming by hearing and hearing by the word of God.

Five Tips to Consider while preaching:

1. If wanting to use a loud speaker, make sure your city doesn't have an ordinance against it.
2. Stay on public property to avoid unnecessary conflict with business owners/ the law.
3. Always temper the Moral Law with Grace and keep the message balanced on both God's hard and soft virtues. Soft virtues are love, mercy, longsuffering, forgivness. Hard virtues are truth, righteousness, Justice, Holiness.
4. Avoid calling out individual spectators sins and focus on speaking generally, be humble.
5. If possible, bring a friend to help you preach, and record yourself to avoid trouble with the law.

Mat 4:17 From that time Jesus began to preach, and to say, Repent: for the kingdom of heaven is at hand.

Mat 10:27 What I tell you in darkness, *that* speak ye in light: and what ye hear in the ear, *that* preach ye upon the housetops.

Mat 24:14 And this gospel of the kingdom shall be preached in all the world for a witness unto all nations; and then shall the end come.

Mar 1:4 John did baptize in the wilderness, and preach the baptism of repentance for the remission of sins.

Mar 6:12 And they went out, and preached that men should repent.

Mar 16:15 And he said unto them, Go ye into all the world, and preach the gospel to every creature.

Luk 24:47 And that repentance and remission of sins should be preached in his name among all nations, beginning at Jerusalem.

Act 5:42 And daily in the temple, and in every house, they ceased not to teach and preach Jesus Christ.

Act 8:25 And they, when they had testified and preached the word of the Lord, returned to Jerusalem, and preached the gospel in many villages of the Samaritans.

Act 13:38 Be it known unto you therefore, men *and* brethren, that through this man is preached unto you the forgiveness of sins:

Act 14:7 And there they preached the gospel.

Act 14:15 And saying, Sirs, why do ye these things? We also are men of like passions with you, and preach unto you that ye should turn from these vanities unto the living God, which made heaven, and earth, and the sea, and all things that are therein:

Act 15:36 And some days after Paul said unto Barnabas, Let us go again and visit our brethren in every city where we have preached the word of the Lord, *and see* how they do.

Rom 10:13 For whosoever shall call upon the name of the Lord shall be saved.

Rom 10:14 How then shall they call on him in whom they have not believed? and how shall they believe in him of whom they have not heard? and how shall they hear without a preacher?

Rom 10:15 And how shall they preach, except they be sent? as it is written, How beautiful are the feet of them that preach the gospel of peace, and bring glad tidings of good things!

Rom 10:17 So then faith *cometh* by hearing, and hearing by the word of God.

1Co 1:18 For the preaching of the cross is to them that perish foolishness; but unto us which are saved it is the power of God.

1Co 1:21 For after that in the wisdom of God the world by wisdom knew not God, it pleased God by the foolishness of preaching to save them that believe.

1Co 1:23 But we preach Christ crucified, unto the Jews a stumblingblock, and unto the Greeks foolishness;

1Co 2:4 And my speech and my preaching *was* not with enticing words of man's wisdom, but in demonstration of the Spirit and of power:

1Co 9:16 For though I preach the gospel, I have nothing to glory of: for necessity is laid upon me; yea, woe is unto me, if I preach not the gospel!

1Co 9:18 What is my reward then? *Verily* that, when I preach the gospel, I may make the gospel of Christ without charge, that I abuse not my power in the gospel.

2Co 4:5 For we preach not ourselves, but Christ Jesus the Lord; and ourselves your servants for Jesus' sake.

Eph 3:8 Unto me, who am less than the least of all saints, is this grace given, that I should preach among the Gentiles the unsearchable riches of Christ;

Php 1:15 Some indeed preach Christ even of envy and strife; and some also of good will:

Php 1:16 The one preach Christ of contention, not sincerely, supposing to add affliction to my bonds:

Php 1:17 But the other of love, knowing that I am set for the defence of the gospel.

Php 1:18 What then? notwithstanding, every way, whether in pretence, or in truth, Christ is preached; and I therein do rejoice, yea, and will rejoice.

1Th 2:16 Forbidding us to speak to the Gentiles that they might be saved, to fill up their sins alway: for the wrath is come upon them to the uttermost.

2Ti 4:2 Preach the word; be instant in season, out of season; reprove, rebuke, exhort with all longsuffering and doctrine.

1Pe 3:19 By which also he went and preached unto the spirits in prison;

1Pe 4:6 For for this cause was the gospel preached also to them that are dead, that they might be judged according to men in the flesh, but live according to God in the spirit.

Rev 14:6 And I saw another angel fly in the midst of heaven, having the everlasting gospel to preach unto them that dwell on the earth, and to every nation, and kindred, and tongue, and people,

Zeal

WEBSTERS REVISED UNABRIDGED Dictionary 1913 "Zeal...

1. Passionate ardor in the pursuit of anything; eagerness in favor of a person or cause; ardent and active interest; engagedness; enthusiasm; fervor. "Ambition varnished o'er with zeal." Milton. "Zeal, the blind conductor of the will." Dryden. "Zeal's never-dying fire." Keble..."

We see in Scripture that Zeal can be a very good thing, there is the account of Phinehas in the old Testament who diverted the Lord's wrath when he smote the man who was messing around with the Midianite woman. Then when have Jesus fulfilling an old testament prophecy about the zeal of the Lord's house. From the book of Revelation we see Jesus admonishing at least one of the churches to be zealous and to repent.

Indeed we also need to watch out for lukewarmness, as things like sports, video games, and chasing the allures of this world can distract us from being focused on Jesus and advancing his kingdom. We as Christians ought to be zealous of good works. I suppose zeal can be a bad thing also when we consider Paul was persecuting the church in his zeal before he was converted.

NUM 25:11 PHINEHAS, the son of Eleazar, the son of Aaron the priest, hath turned my wrath away from the children of Israel, while he was zealous for my sake among them, that I consumed not the children of Israel in my jealousy.

Psa 69:9 For the zeal of thine house hath eaten me up; and the reproaches of them that reproached thee are fallen upon me.

Psa 119:139 My zeal hath consumed me, because mine enemies have forgotten thy words.

Isa 9:7 Of the increase of *his* government and peace *there shall be* no end, upon the throne of David, and upon his kingdom, to order it, and to establish it with judgment and with justice from henceforth even for ever. The zeal of the LORD of hosts will perform this.

Isa 59:17 For he put on righteousness as a breastplate, and an helmet of salvation upon his head; and he put on the garments of vengeance *for* clothing, and was clad with zeal as a cloke.

Joh 2:17 And his disciples remembered that it was written, The zeal of thine house hath eaten me up.

Act 21:20 And when they heard *it,* they glorified the Lord, and said unto him, Thou seest, brother, how many thousands of Jews there are which believe; and they are all zealous of the law:

Act 22:3 I am verily a man *which am* a Jew, born in Tarsus, *a city* in Cilicia, yet brought up in this city at the feet of Gamaliel, *and* taught according to the perfect manner of the law of the fathers, and was zealous toward God, as ye all are this day.

Rom 10:2 For I bear them record that they have a zeal of God, but not according to knowledge.

1Co 14:12 Even so ye, forasmuch as ye are zealous of spiritual *gifts,* seek that ye may excel to the edifying of the church.

2Co 7:11 For behold this selfsame thing, that ye sorrowed after a godly sort, what carefulness it wrought in you, yea, *what* clearing of yourselves, yea, *what* indignation, yea, *what* fear, yea, *what* vehement desire, yea, *what* zeal, yea, *what* revenge! In all *things* ye have approved yourselves to be clear in this matter.

Gal 1:14 And profited in the Jews' religion above many my equals in mine own nation, being more exceedingly zealous of the traditions of my fathers.

Php 3:6 Concerning zeal, persecuting the church; touching the righteousness which is in the law, blameless.

Tit 2:14 Who gave himself for us, that he might redeem us from all iniquity, and purify unto himself a peculiar people, zealous of good works.

Rev 3:19 As many as I love, I rebuke and chasten: be zealous therefore, and repent.

Don't miss out!

Visit the website below and you can sign up to receive emails whenever Justin Horn publishes a new book. There's no charge and no obligation.

https://books2read.com/r/B-A-KAVIB-YNKED

BOOKS 2 READ

Connecting independent readers to independent writers.